Growing Up with a Crazy
Italian Mother

Growing Up with a Crazy Italian Mother

Tony Tripodi

iUniverse, Inc.

New York Lincoln Shanghai

Growing Up with a Crazy Italian Mother

iUniverse books may be ordered through booksellers or by contacting:

iUniverse
2021 Pine Lake Road, Suite 100
Lincoln, NE 68512
www.iuniverse.com
1-800-Authors (1-800-288-4677)

ISBN-13: 978-0-595-39607-8 (pbk)
ISBN-13: 978-0-595-84010-6 (ebk)
ISBN-10: 0-595-39607-0 (pbk)
ISBN-10: 0-595-84010-8 (ebk)

Printed in the United States of America

Contents

1

Introduction

This book is not about a joyful, effervescent Italian woman who danced the Tarantella around the house, singing songs with her children about the beauties of Italy. It's about a woman from Calabria, Italy, who partook of an arranged marriage in America, subsequently experiencing the immigrant life in a strange land and coping with the shame and degradation of mental illness. Growing Up with a Crazy Italian Mother is also about me, her last and youngest child, and her strengths and weaknesses that influenced my growth and development as a second generation Italian American.

Having recently retired from my position as a dean and professor of a college of social work at a large Midwestern university, I decided to delve into how and in what way my mother influenced my life. I delayed writing about this for 45 years because it was too painful to think about. My mother, Christina, was an Italian immigrant in the aftermath of World War I, and she was diagnosed as a paranoid schizophrenic in the early 1930's, courtesy of the California Department of Mental Hygiene, which was intent on cleaning and altering the woeful minds of the mentally ill. To understand how I dealt with my mother's illness and how I learned about it represents for me a painful, although sometimes humorous, journey of revelation, insecurities, and self doubts.

I hesitated to write this book due to the mental pain and anguish I encountered as I struggled to recall a life with my mother that spanned form 1932, when I was born, to 1959, when she died. Remembering the past and discovering sources of influence on the way I lived might have been therapeutic, but it also opened wounds that I suppressed for many years. Hopefully, the story of how my mother and I coped with her parenting, immigrant status, and mental illness might be helpful for others who have mentally ill family members. However, this book is not intended to be a comprehensive text; rather, it is a journey I took back in time to learn something about the interaction between my mother and myself.

Up until 1959 when I was employed by the California Department of Mental Hygiene as a research technician, I had an idea that some of my mother's actions were bizarre; but I didn't know, or rather refused to admit, that she was mentally ill. I thought she was peculiar, eccentric, and a believer of many cultural superstitions, such as the mal'occhio, the evil eye, which one would do well to avoid. None of my siblings spoke of or even acknowledged mental illness in the family. After all, crazy people were to be shunned; they were bad, and it was shameful to be associated with them. I discovered Christina's diagnosis and her attempted suicide when I was working on a research project. At work we were trying to discover the effectiveness of ataractic drugs administered to patients in the State of California mental health system. This revelation of my mother's illness marks the beginning of my journey. It is followed by conversations with my mother at her death bed. Then, based on discussions with siblings and my recollections of the past, I left the death bed to reflect on my mother's struggles with immigration, mental illness, and poverty to her acquisition of property and her relationships with her grandchildren. I discuss my mother's migration from Italy to Ithaca, New York, and perceptions of her life with her first husband and their three children, my siblings. This is followed by her abrupt departure from Ithaca with her children and a new man in her life, my father. Christina was divorced in Reno, Nevada, and also married my father there. Six months later, I, a 9-pound baby boy was born. I don't know whether I was considered as a premature baby. If so, I probably would have weighed about 14 or 15 pounds at birth, destined to be a tackle in the National Football League. My sister said that I had a twin brother who died at birth. I couldn't imagine my mother dealing with all 18 pounds of baby. However, it could have been possible, particularly after recently hearing that my brother, Tommy, weighed 16 pounds at birth. Tommy became a small-sized baseball player rather than a tackle. Obviously, I wasn't premature. I discuss the early years of my life, walks with my mother, and talks about her wanting to commit suicide—talks that I simply forgot or that I repressed. I also discuss the impact of my father's death that occurred one month before Pearl Harbor and World War II.

All of those events plus her marriages and my breaking away to go to college are considered with an eye toward uncovering the positive and negative influences my mother, Christina, had on my life. I'm an ordinary person who has been moderately successful in his career, and I recognize that this book is primarily based on my recollections of events that occurred from 44 to 72 years ago. To the extent that my perceptions are accurate, this is a memoir. On the other hand, some of my perceptions may be inaccurate; and to that degree, this is a work of fiction. Nevertheless, the flavor of my upbringing by my crazy Italian mother will be evident.

2

Revelation

I received my master's degree in psychiatric social work from the University of California at Berkeley in 1958. While at Berkeley, I interned at the Veterans Administration Neuropsychiatric Hospital in Palo Alto, California, concentrating in psychiatric social work as well as social research. Working with psychotic patients in planning for their discharges from the hospital, I felt uneasy and often had quite severe headaches. I was much more comfortable engaging in group therapy and in assisting psychologists in their research on learning theory and behavior modification. I enjoyed the cognitive aspects of my work, but found it difficult to discuss the patients' feelings and interpersonal interactions. I had no idea why I had those difficulties, nor did I, at that time, know they were possibly related to my mother's mental illness. However, I excelled at research and statistics and was offered a job as a research social worker at the hospital in Palo Alto. I turned down that job and accepted a job as a research technician with the California Department of Mental Hygiene in Sacramento. The job was designed for a Ph.D. researcher, so I felt it was an opportunity to learn more about research prior to entering a doctoral program in social research or biostatistics.

I enjoyed the substance of the job in Sacramento. I was responsible for writing monthly reports on mental retardation and in conducting analyses of patients' lengths of stay in hospitals. I took courses in statistics and data processing and learned a great deal. However, I soon discovered that the director of the statistical bureau in which I worked did not speak well of his employees, indicating that the reasons the bureau was behind in reports was due to the incompetence of his employees. He claimed that he was a perfectionist. That was why every report that I turned in was criticized to the nth degree, and he, Mr. Morgan, rewrote it and told me to work on it some more. After a month of this non-productive compulsivity, I decided to not change the report at all but to hand him back his own corrections a week later, acting as if I rewrote the report. Again, he criticized the writing, I told him it was his writing. This infuriated him. He said that like his son I would soon learn to appreciate his supervision. I responded that I was an employee, not his son; and this infuriated him even more. It was obvious to all of the employees that the director, himself, was holding up the work. He told his boss that no one could produce good, scholarly work, and he also told us. This inspired a colleague and myself to design a research project, carry it out, and submit it for publication to the <u>American Journal of Public Health</u>. Our reasoning was that if we could get our work accepted in what the bureau regarded as a prestigious journal, we could refute the boss' notion of incompetence. Fortunately, for us and unfortunately for him, the article was accepted for publication; the upshot of it was that the higher administration began to wonder about the competency of the director.

It was in this atmosphere of interesting work but strained employer-employee relations in the department of mental hygiene that I wondered whether my mother had ever been in the State of California's mental hygiene system. This was due to the fact that we were putting materials from all patients as far back as the 1930's and beyond on IBM cards in order to facilitate subsequent data analysis. Somewhere in the back of my mind, I must have questioned whether or not Christina had ever been a patient. Hence, in the early months of 1959, I looked up my mother's name.

I found IBM cards for her! They indicated that she was placed on observation after an attempted suicide when I was a young boy of six. My mother was diagnosed as a paranoid schizophrenic! In spite of my education, my immediate thoughts were self centered. Recalling the hopelessness and chronicity of those diagnosed as paranoid schizophrenic at the Veterans Administration hospital in Palo Alto, I wondered whether my mother's diagnosis was correct and whether or not I was destined to become mentally ill. I wanted to tear up the IBM cards to hide her mental illness, reacting at the time with all the stigma against mental illness that I could muster. In 1959, the notion of schizophrenogenic mothers was in vogue. The idea was that schizophrenic mothers by their own bizarre behaviors could instill schizophrenic behaviors in their children. This idea was subsequently refuted in later years, but it led me to question my own sanity as well as wondering whether my own difficulties in interpersonal relationships were influenced by my mother.

I recently read the book, <u>Growing Up with a Schizophrenic Mother</u>, by Margaret J. Brown and Doris Parker Roberts (McFarland and Company, Inc. Publishers, Jefferson, NC and London, 2000). The authors studied 44 adult children of schizophrenic mothers, and it apparently was common for the children to report shame, fear, feelings of abandonment, and difficulties in interpersonal relationships. Moreover, the book, <u>My Parents' Keeper: Adult Children of the Emotionally Disturbed</u>, by Eva Marian Brown (Edited by Nina Sononberg, 1980, New Harbinger Publications, Oakland, California) indicated that these adult children experienced fears of craziness, insecurity, and difficulty in getting in touch with their own feelings. If I had read those books at the time and/or discussed my thoughts and feelings with a psychotherapist, I might not have experienced as much anxiety and fear as I did. I felt that I was alone and that I, too, would become mentally ill. The revelation of Christina's mental illness jolted my memory, and a flood of events from the past entered my mind. To deal with thoughts of crazy interactions between my mother and myself, I tried to suppress them. However, I began to recall her psychotic symptoms and my fear of going crazy. For many years, I tried to suppress these thoughts. To some extent, I succeeded. Nevertheless, throughout my life, from 1959 to the present time, I gathered impressions and information from others about my mother's behaviors, particularly from my brothers and sister. And, it is only recently that I have been able to go back in time, recalling and attempting to understand how my life was shaped by my mother's attitudes and behaviors toward me.

Within months of the revelation, my mother died. She was in the advanced stages of diabetes, blind for four years from glaucoma, and suffering from gangrene, with the loss of a foot. Prior to Christina's admission to Mercy Hospital, my sister took care of her, providing her with a large, special room in her house. My mother had mellowed at the age of 62. She turned on the television to keep her company, and she was thrilled when talking with her grandchildren. She smiled and spoke humorously of her life in Italy as well as in American. Christina was especially happy when talking with her Mexican friend, Esther. My mother spoke in Italian, and Esther spoke in Spanish. They got along famously, making fun of people who used to work where they did, at the Southern Pacific Railroad. It was at her death bed that she recalled and relived her psychotic behaviors.

3

Death Bed

Christina was hospitalized at Sutter Mercy Hospital and was in a great deal of pain after her gangrenous foot had been amputated. It was days prior to her death that I spent four hours alone with her in a hospital room for intensive care. Drugged with morphine, she talked incessantly about many of the sad events in her life. I was so overwhelmed with anxiety and fear that I resorted to defensive, psychological mechanisms of depersonalization, compartmentalization, intellectualization, and avoidance. This, at least, allowed me to be able to sit with her without screaming for mercy, as if it were my fault for her mental illness, my mea culpa rather than her sua culpa. I suppressed my feelings and acted very clinically, noting her behaviors and expressions, trying to relate them with her to the past. I thought of her as a patient, depersonalizing my own feelings, observing myself interact with my mother—trying to be comforting and helpful, yet suppressing the fear that I would be like her. I wondered if the chemical changes from her pain and the morphine might have triggered the apparent psychotic state at her deathbed, leading her to recall previous psychotic episodes in her life. Ironically, I was engaged in research regarding the effectiveness of drugs aimed at counter balancing the possible chemical imbalances in schizophrenics. And, sadly, I wondered whether she might have been helped by the new drugs that were being produced and researched.

It was in my mothers' ramblings that she verified what I learned about her from the IBM cards in the California Department of Mental Hygiene. At her death bed, what was uppermost in her mind was that she wanted me to tell the doctors to kill her. She said her amputated foot was thrown in the garbage, so why shouldn't her whole body be thrown away. It was very difficult for me, but I told her I would tell the doctors what she said. However, I told her that I didn't think they would kill her; they would try to make her more comfortable. Most of us in the 1950's were not sensitive to the patient's right to life or death, but if I could go back in time, I would not have wanted to grant my mother's request. After all, it would not have been a good Catholic thing to do.

Speaking of a Catholic thing not to do, two priests within a span of a couple of hours gave my mother two sacraments of extreme unction. The Catholic religion played a very important role in the lives of Italian immigrants, and I'm sure my mother would have felt that a place in heaven was assured for her with two extreme unctions. This, in spite of the fact she was theoretically ex-communicated due to her multiple marriages. The works of the two priests provided a way for me to discharge some of my pent-up feelings. I was angry, saying to the second priest, "For Christ's sake, how many extreme unctions does a person have to endure?" Of course, the priest was just doing his job, but he didn't seem to be aware that extreme unction had already been administered by the first priest. They apparently worked in shifts, reading notes about the patient, my mother, who was listed as in critical condition. The first priest read the notes and subsequently administered the sacrament of extreme unction, the final sacrament in a Catholic person's life. Apparently, he did not record his action. Later, the second priest, reading the same notes, also administered extreme unction. I have no idea as to whether it was an instance of double jeopardy, double indemnity, or double or nothing in the stakes for entry into heaven.

From her death bed, my mother recalled her suicide attempt, yelling and screaming that she was going to commit suicide. She spoke about how she was going to do it; either by lying on the railroad tracks until a train would come and run over her, or by throwing herself in the American River and drowning—a drowning that would be ironic for an immigrant in the promised land of America.

Christina told me that doctors threw poison in her hair, as she spit in a handkerchief and scratched her head. I then remembered that this is what she told me throughout my childhood—sometimes when she was angry, sometimes with no warning at all like the sudden appearance of a gale on a calm, placid day. She said people tried to tell her she was crazy. Au contraire, she thought they were crazy, united in a conspiracy to keep her in a mental hospital. So far as I could understand her Calabrian dialect of Italian, my mother was unhappy due to my father's philandering as well as the responsibilities she had borne to take care of her four children. Like most Italian women who migrated to America, the burden of child rearing and tending to domestic chores fell on my mother. Although she could speak a broken English, Christina only talked of her olfactory and tactile delusions in Italian. Everything smelled bad, and the poison led her to pull her hair and expectorate. She was trying to get rid of the poison in her system.

I received more information about my father. According to my mother, he cavorted with other women. Of course, she said my father loved me, just like she did; and I was very much like my father. Then, all of a sudden, fears of both mental illness and philandering were in my vision. This came to me after I was divorced the previous year due to a liaison I had with another woman. Was it true? Like father, like son! Like mother, like son! This made me think that I was doomed to be a philandering schizophrenic, or was it a schizophrenic philanderer?

I willed myself to suppress those feelings. Although I felt like I was dying, it was my mother who was dying. It was her life that I was trying to respect. I loved her and admired how hard she worked to make life easier for me. Her goal seemed to be one of most immigrants: to enable their offspring to live in a better world than they did. I knew my mother loved me. I was said to be her favorite, but her love was one of an over supply of food, inconsistent affection, accusations of poisoning her, spankings, and lots of yelling.

Christina cried a lot during those four hours. She talked about her unfortunate life, telling me she loved all of her children. Just as I didn't cry at my father's death, I couldn't cry about my mother's passing. I pushed the feelings of loneliness, lack of love, and despair deep into an abyss which I hoped to avoid. My psychological defense mechanisms hardened me to death, to treat it as common place. Yet deep down inside my very being I was angry that God placed such a burden on my mother and on me. What was the point of all of this misery? Did God really exist, and was Jesus perpetually dying for our sins? Rather than being bitter, I was apprehensive of what the future would bring. My mother was proud of me when I graduated from high school with scholarships and numerous awards in science, citizenship, and honor societies. And, I desired that she would continually be proud of my accomplishments; so I definitely wanted to pursue doctoral studies in statistics and social research, hoping that in spirit she would be proud of my accomplishments and thinking that not all of her life was in vain.

My mother's funeral was a sad event. All of her children and grandchildren mourned their loss. To me, it was very touching that her Mexican friend, Esther, came to the funeral. Perhaps, it was a tribute to Christina's increasing tolerance of other ethnic and minority groups. When I was a student at Sutter Junior High School, she constantly told me how bad it was to associate with Mexicans even though they were one step above Portuguese immigrants on the Christina scale of social approval. Ironically, my sister's first husband, Frank, was of Portuguese descent, as was my brother Tommy's wife. Naturally, I drew her wrath by giving away a radio I made to a Portuguese boy who lived across the train tracks in a pretty filthy farm, where humans, animals, and their feces seemed to commingle. Christina didn't want the radio, so I gave it to someone lower on her social approval scale.

My mother's funeral was symptomatic of upward mobility and the rise of acculturation among Italian immigrants in America. When my father died in 1941, he was buried in the poor section of St. Mary's Cemetery in Sacramento. In contrast, Christina was entombed in a vault in the nicer part of the cemetery in 1959. It was she who achieved a higher socioeconomic status by her sheer will, working night and day at two jobs during World War II, saving her money and investing in several apartment buildings.

It was amazing that my mother's illness did not stop her from functioning well in several different jobs, and from buying and renting out apartments. Of course, it is noteworthy that she had my sister do a great deal of the work. Unlike many people diagnosed as schizophrenic, she was able to deal with practical, realistic, financial problems in a functional way. However, she was not repeatedly hospitalized like the schizophrenic mother discussed in the book, Growing Up with a Schizophrenic Mother; and this freedom from the culture of hospitalized schizophrenics as well as less severity of the illness may have helped her to increase her social functioning.

The revelations of Christina's psychosis and her death bed wishes stimulated me to delve in the past and discover how she influenced me over time. Her influence was positive such as a strong work ethic and negative as in inconsistent parenting amidst words of love and threats of death. In the remaining chapters, I explore what I perceive as positive and negative influences of my mother on my life.

4

Immigration

After the end of World War I, many Italians migrated to America in search of a life without poverty. Approximately ten years after immigration to Ellis Island in New York, the Italians, like all Americans, found themselves struggling to survive among the Great Depression. As an example of the plight of Italian immigrants, Pietro Di Donato's novel, <u>Christ in Concrete</u>, published in 1939 (New American Library) depicts the struggles of brick layers and their families in New York City. In addition, he described cultural characteristics of Italian immigrants in America: hard work, sharing food and wine with families, relying heavily on prayers to God and the advice of Catholic priests, and the power of the fine Italian hand in embroidery, gardening, cooking, laying brick, and building concrete structures.

It was the atmosphere of escaping poverty in Italy to one of finding poverty in America that permeated my mother's early experiences as an immigrant. A woman in her early 20's, my mother, Christina, embarked for America to visit her uncle in Ithaca, New York. Little did she know that her uncle arranged for her to marry her cousin who was also from the province of Calabria. It was an arranged marriage. No matter how much she cried at the prospect of marriage, she had to marry her cousin. This was because her life was in jeopardy if she didn't agree to the marriage. In essence, she was a trafficked slave. Her job was to bear children and to supply and prepare food for her family. Feeling she had no choice, she moved to Ithaca, where her older sister, Angelina, had migrated several years earlier.

In celebration of the positive aspects of immigration, I was thrilled when Lee Iacocca pushed the idea of an immigrant wall with names of the immigrants on Ellis Island, in view of the Statue of Liberty. I made sure that my mother's and father's names were on that wall: Christina Maria Grandinetti and Nicola Tripodi. And, I have always been proud of their names perpetually in New York harbor where eager and hopeful people first eyed the symbol of America, the Statue of Liberty. The immigrant museum on Ellis Island describes the clothing, baggage, and hardship of people stacked in ships, mostly below deck and subject to the motions of the sea, inducing vomiting and illness in many of the passengers. My mother talked about the cramped quarters in the ship. She and other passengers became very sick. However, Christina also regarded the experience as an adventure; she was excited about the idea of America.

When I was a young man in college, I asked my mother if she had ever been in love. I suppose the question was a result of the skepticism and cynicism I rapidly acquired at the University of California at Berkeley, or it might have been my curiosity as to whether or not she had experienced love. The question might have seemed silly and out of context for a woman who had been married four times; but, surprisingly, she answered it, not by referring to any of her marriages which seemed more like liaisons of convenience, but by referring to a young man she met on the ship to America. According to her, they spent a great deal of time together on the deck, feeling the mist of the Atlantic Ocean on their faces and watching the stars brightly shining in the sky. Christina said they were in love; but, as I understood it, she had to honor her duty to visit her uncle in Ithaca. She and her lover parted ways at Ellis Island.

Christina went from the impossible dream of young lovers to the harsh realities of the "town" and "gown" in Ithaca. The "town" was symbolically represented by Italian immigrants who worked in whatever jobs they could find, often in dreary conditions and long hours at the gun factory. Cornell University, a world class university with outstanding faculty and students, represented the "gown" of privilege and success. This town and gown feature has been dramatized in sociological studies of New Haven, Connecticut, home of Yale University and of many Italian immigrants in the 1920's and 1930's. During those years, it was typical of great universities to have sociologists who studied American society and the divide between gown and town, the haves and the have nots.

My mother knew nothing about sociology and American society. She gave birth to three children, my sister, Phil, and my brothers, Tommy and Joe. Working hard in domestic work for little pay, Christina also raised rabbits, pigeons, chickens, vegetables, and, of course, her three children. She was quick to employ the skills gained from her peasant background in Italy. She reared animals, and then killed them by a snap of the neck or by a rabbit punch. Years later I saw her efficiently kill pigeons, rabbits, and chickens; and then prepare them for cooking. She cooked multiple course dinners with soups, pasta, meat, potatoes, and fish. Dinner was a time to talk, but it was also a time for drunkenness and verbal abuse on the part of her husband. Often times her husband was so drunk that he couldn't report to work at the gun factory. The story I heard was that my mother substituted for him so he wouldn't lose his job. She also took in boarders to raise more money for the family.

It must have been difficult for her to attempt to learn a new language at the same time as working in multiple tasks and jobs to keep the family together. Just like the Italians depicted in <u>Christ in Concrete</u>, my mother placed a high value on her family. Rumor has it that she rented a chicken coop in Ithaca to people who had no homes. This was during the Great Depression; and life in America was not any rosier than it had been in the arid lands of Southern Italy. It was during that time that she met my father, one of her boarders, who was from Reggio, Calabria, whereas she was from San Pietro L'Apostolo (St. Peter the Apostle), also in Calabria. My mother packed all of their clothes and with her children and my father traveled in 1932 to Reno, Nevada. They lived in Reno for six months so she could get a divorce prior to marrying my father. They then moved to Sacramento, California.

Christina didn't become a citizen of the United States in her stay at Ithaca. She was too busy working. In addition to her other chores, she made blankets, tablecloths, doilies, and clothes for her children. Worse of all, which apparently wasn't uncommon for Italian women at that time, Christina suffered a great deal of verbal abuse. Imbued with la testa di Calabria (the Calabrian temperament), my mother was strong willed and stubborn. It was these traits that evidently led her to seize the opportunity to travel across the country to rid herself of the life she endured in Ithaca.

I never knew whether Christina found any happiness in her first ten years in America. I assume that she did not find the proverbial pot of gold at the end of the rainbow that filtered down to Ithaca. It is clear to me that my mother had to be adventurous to migrate again to another unknown place, California.

Sometimes, I wonder whether Christina would have been happier if she would have run off with the man she met on the ship to America. Fixed marriages were essentially a form of slavery that many women endured. Italian men were dominant, and they ruled over their wives and children.

5

Early Years in Sacramento

I was born at the county hospital in Sacramento, and I became the baby of a new family of six. Imagine what it would have been like if I had a twin brother, increasing the family size to seven? My sister, Phil, said I had a twin brother named Sam who fell off the delivery table and died. At least, Phil didn't say that I was selfish, wanting to be THE FAMILY BABY, pushing him to his death.

I was fed a lot of spaghetti, and I obviously enjoyed it; for I was a very fat infant. It was apparent to my brothers and sister that I was getting a great deal of attention, whereas they were feeling the wrath of my father's strictness. Everyone at the table had to finish all of the food on their plates, that is everyone except me, my father's one and only child. Everyone complied except my brother, Joe. Joe was ingenious in finding ways to dispose of the food he didn't like. For example, he hated horse beans (big lima beans). Gradually he would slip all of the beans into his pants pockets, discarding them later after my father was out of sight. Perhaps, this deceptiveness was an early indication that Joe would become a well-known gambler, deceiving those he played with as well as the police.

Nick, my father, worked as a laborer for the Western Pacific Railroad. His ambition was to be a plumber. But, in those years between 1932 and 1938 the remnants of the Stock Market Crash of 1929 were still being felt; and my father was fortunate to have a job. Christina, as was the case in Ithaca, was again using skills she developed in Italy to take care of her family. Judging by the food she made available, it didn't seem like poverty. My mother planted vegetables and tended almond, walnut, and fig trees, drying their fruits in the warm California sunshine. In addition, she raised pigeons, chickens, and rabbits that became the source of many of our meals. Once a year, Nick would buy a pig. Christina would then kill it and make use of every available organ to make food: pickled pig's feet, sausage made from pig's meat put in the pig's intestines, tongue, brain, and so forth. Possibly, I was a secret Jew, a Sephardic Jew; for as a child, I couldn't stomach any of the pig's meat. Since we raised rabbits and pigeons, I gave names to them. There was no way I could eat pets that were cute and cuddly. Chickens were neither cute nor cuddly, so I didn't consider them as pets. Consequently, I had no trouble eating chicken or beef from cows I did not see. My mother told me that rabbits and pigeons (squab) tasted just like chicken, but I still couldn't eat them. In my teenage years as I developed into a smart ass I retorted to my mother that it didn't matter that rabbits and pigeons tasted like chicken because I simply didn't like the taste of chicken. However, I did love the bread my mother baked, meatballs, and the spicy salami and pepperoni that were always available.

When I was two to three years old, I spent the days at a daycare center, which was very close to the Western Pacific train tracks. It was exciting to see my father riding the rails on hand carts.

I don't remember too much about my father. I knew he was fond of me. If I were playing in an alley about a block away from our house, I would come running as soon as I heard his whistle and his shouting of "Nino," an affectionate name for a baby boy. One Sunday afternoon, he took my mother and me in his Model A Ford to a farm to buy grapes for making wine. He made three barrels of strong, red wine every year. Wine was always available at the dinner table, and occasionally I had a sip. My mother and father consumed large quantities of wine at each meal.

Nick had some strange eating habits. He would put a raw egg in a glass of wine and drink the mixture; he put salt on raw meat and ate it; and he submerged bread that my mother made in a concoction of olive oil, salt, and pepper. I don't know whether or not his diet had to do with his low count of white blood cells and the leukemia that rendered him physically challenged in the last two years of his life, when he was in various hospitals in Sacramento, Portola, and San Francisco. I tried the raw meat with salt and thought it wasn't fit for animals, let alone young boys. I didn't try the wine and egg; but I loved, and still do, bread dipped in virgin olive oil with lots of pepper sprinkled on it.

Strangely, I don't remember any interactions between my mother and father. When my godparents visited, my mother was charming, exhibiting a great memory of old people and things in the "old country." While my mother was reminiscing about Italy, Nick concentrated on playing cards and drinking the wine he made.

My father essentially ruled over us children as my mother kept on serving food. Christina toiled for hours, making bread, soup, and sauces for spaghetti. Typical of Italian peasants in America, she was careful to preserve food by canning tomatoes, peaches, and apricots. Nick made sure that we would leave no food on our plates. This may have been due to his fears about the Depression, and it also could have been due to the impending doom facing him and our family through his illness.

Perhaps, my father had little interaction with Christina because he spent much time with other women. And, that possibly could have led to her alleged suicide attempt. When I took walks with my mother, she often spoke about suicide.

Our house, where now stands a school for homeless children, was one house away from a 20 foot high levee. At the top of the levee were train tracks which were traversed by Southern Pacific passenger and freight trains. There was a long road, about one block long, that went up to and over the tracks to a gravel company situated by the American River. Directly across the tracks was a hobo camp where many homeless men dwelt, with make shift shelters and fires burning to keep them warm. Nearby were acres of woods with trees laced with mushrooms. Further along there was a farm where a poor Portuguese family lived. The farm was close to a dump, and it always reeked with the odor of cow dung.

My mother and I took walks to the river, which was about one mile from the railroad tracks. During those walks my mother picked mushrooms that she would fry for evening meals. Italians seem to have a knack for discerning poisonous from non-poisonous mushrooms. I remember thinking the ones with pretty colors were good; they were, of course, poisonous! Even in adulthood, when engaged in mushroom hunting with Italians who participated in a seminar on social research in Molosco, Italy, I couldn't distinguish poisonous from non-poisonous mushrooms. It was unfortunate because I considered my self Italian. Perhaps, I was more of an urban Italian than a rural Italian. However, my mother definitely knew how to pick edible mushrooms.

On the way to the river we also walked by the dump and searched for any items that were salvageable. I don't remember ever finding anything of value. My mother rummaged through the trash in the hope and anticipation of finding discarded treasures. Near the gravel company, the American River had many eddies. People were warned not to swim there due to the dangerous undertow. Paradoxically, many of my happier days as a teenager were taken up by swimming in the American River. Other boys and I would swing out on a rope tied to one of the trees on the bank of the river, letting go, and plunging into the water. Tanning in the sun was a way to pass time in the day. There were shallower parts in the river but with a very strong current. I learned how to swim by reading a Boy Scout book on swimming at the library and then trying out the strokes in the American

River. The current of the river helped me to think I was actually swimming since it moved me along rapidly.

On these walks with my mother, she spoke of committing suicide in either of two different ways: by throwing herself in the river, getting caught in a whirlpool and drowning; or by laying on the railroad tracks, waiting for a train to come and run over her. She said that her life was no good; it was unbearable, and one day she would kill herself. I don't know what I felt at the time, but as I write this I can feel the anxiety at the thought of suicide and of how difficult life must have been for my mother. Yet, I was about six years old and had little comprehension of what she was talking about. As a child, I was very quiet, simply listening but not talking. In fact, my sister seems to take pleasure in telling me that everyone thought I was dumb because I never talked. I thought that people repeated the same thing over and over, and there wasn't much to say. This was similar to a class I took in graduate school. The other students and the instructor seemed to invent different ways to say the same thing; and that led me to be silent.

I didn't ask my mother why she wanted to commit suicide. It was, in my perception as a child, telling me she wanted to leave me alone. Although she said she loved me, the fact that she spoke about leaving through a self-imposed death must have been very confusing. In one sense, I might have thought my mother was simply trying to get attention. I know I told her not to lay on the tracks or jump in the river, but I don't recall my exact words or the feelings of horror I must have had. When she talked about suicide, I did ask her to hold my hand. I either wanted to hold her back from suicide, or I wanted her to take me along. I just didn't want to be alone.

Several years later, after my father died, I was caught smoking cigarettes at a baseball park where my brother, Tommy, was playing baseball. As a consequence, I received a series of spankings from my mother and my siblings. I ran away, but only for an hour. I ran up to the railroad tracks and lay down, waiting for a train to come. I didn't really want to commit suicide. I wanted my family to come up and rescue me, saying they loved me. Could that have been what my mother wanted to hear, somebody saying they loved her? It was an attention-getting device on my part, but I didn't have either the courage or the stupidity to compete the act. After lying on the tracks for a while, I heard people yelling for me, "Nino, Nino." I came running down from the tracks, saying nothing about what I had been doing. I was undoubtedly influenced by my mother in what I probably thought was attention-getting behavior in her talks about suicide. However, I don't know whether I sensed anything about her "suicide attempt" that I uncovered while working at the California State Department of Mental Hygiene. A different scenario might have been one in which she argued with my father, yelling that he was poisoning her and saying she would kill herself. He might have said, "Go ahead and do it." Upon reflection he might have worried that she actually would do it; so he called the police who took her to a state mental hospital for observation. If that were the situation, she also would have pulled her hair and beat her chest with her fists in a fit of rage? Had I known of this (and maybe I did?), it would have been frightening, convincing me that any love toward me was fragile and that I was destined to be unhappy and alone.

As my father became ill and my mother had to take on more responsibility in eking out a living and caring for us children, she became stronger. I rarely heard talk of suicide. And, when I did hear such talk, I perceived it as a manipulative device. "If you don't stop arguing with me, I'll kill myself!" That was a refrain I heard from her as I told her to "go ahead and do it," perhaps in a manner consistent with how my father might have reacted. She obviously didn't commit suicide.

My father, Nick, was a patient in several different hospitals. When he was at Mercy Hospital, approximately one and one half miles from Marshall Elementary School where I was a student, I surprised him by walking from school to the hospital to see him. I felt positive regard and love from him. I had no idea that he had leukemia, nor did I know what it was, other than a diminution in white blood cells. I thought he would be hospitalized only for a short time. My mother cried a lot then. The hospital at Portola was supposed to be for his convalescence. According to my brother Tommy, Nick thought the fresh air at Portola would help him. In reality, it was another stop en route to the hospital in San Francisco, where he was to die November 4, 1941. Strange as it may seem, I was most fascinated in Portola by the lizards darting about the wooden walkway to my father's room. The hospitals always smelled of chemicals and of a false sterility due to the multiple cleanings of the floors. I felt lonely when visiting him in the hospitals. I hated their stark, dreary nature and the secrets that were kept about my father's health.

Trips to the hospital in San Francisco opened up my eyes to the bay and the sea. We traveled by train which stopped in Oakland; then we transferred to a ferry boat that took us to the Ferry Building in San Francisco. I enjoyed the ride on the ferry boat, as well as looking at the sea gulls in their scavenging ventures. I don't think Jonathan Seagull was in that group of greedy birds. Many years later as a young Navy journalist aboard the U.S.S. Wasp, I would sail from the San Francisco Bay under the Golden Gate Bridge to the Pacific Ocean and beyond. My mother didn't enjoy the ferry boat ride at all. She was severely stern, oblivious to the motions of the sea. Her thoughts were probably of the new responsibilities she would have after my father's death. I was not involved in any discussions about the status of his health. I felt numb. There was little to smile about. It felt as if we were walking under a dark cloud that would soon submerge us in a blanket of water. My mother was sad, crying from time to time. However, I didn't know why she was crying. I apparently had no idea that my father's prognosis for staying alive was not good. Perhaps, I heard about the prognosis, but I didn't want to hear it. At any rate, reality crept in with his death.

My father's funeral was like an unsolved mystery. I didn't understand it. My father was dressed in a brown suit, and he felt like stone. People said I should kiss him, but I couldn't. I felt like he was and wasn't my father. Many prayers were said in Italian, Latin, and English. I dreaded hearing the ominous sound of the organ when the mass ended. As I write, I recall how much I preferred the Italian and Latin masses to the current hip hop kind of masses where they're great efforts to be contemporary, cosmopolitan, and ecumenical. Masses in a language I didn't know helped to give me a sense of the mystery of the Holy Trinity: the Father, the Son, and the Holy Ghost. It was the Holy Ghost that was mysterious. Perhaps, that's why it was changed to the Holy Spirit in later years, to be less mysterious and more comprehensible.

There was a great deal of dirt that surrounded the rectangular hole that was dug in the ground. When the casket was lowered, my mother wailed hysterically, pulling her hair and sobbing. This evidently was not abnormal behavior for Italian women who lost their husbands. To me, it was frightening. I felt so terribly lonely. The night after his burial, my mother showed me the cross that had been used in the funeral. I dreamt that my father had come back and was alive. It wasn't like the resurrection of Jesus on Easter Sunday; it was like an everyday occurrence of seeing my father as a healthy, young man. I went to my mother's bedroom to tell her I saw him. I didn't understand how he could still be alive after he was supposed to be dead. At that moment, my mother showed her love for me by comforting, hugging, and telling me he was not alive. She said she knew he was going to die the night she went to a carnival. A bird flew to various parts of a circle that had printed fortunes and pulled out one for each customer. The bird's fortune for my mother was that her husband was going to die.

My mother, like many immigrants from Southern Italy, was superstitious. She believed in the evil eye and, unlike Sigmund Freud, believed that the meaning of dreams could be interpreted. She had a book that gave meanings for different dreams, and she believed the various interpretations. I don't know whether she interpreted the meaning of the dream I had about seeing my father. However, she said something like, "He came to see you to say goodbye since you didn't kiss him." I felt like I must have done something wrong. When I was a young man I spent several sessions in psychotherapy to try understand relationship problems I had. It wasn't too helpful because I acted like I was a good student, saying things I thought the therapist wanted to hear. I received compliments from him as to how I improved very rapidly and was not in the need of further therapy. The unsuccessful part of my therapy in the eyes of the therapist may have been that I couldn't pursue the possibility that I was angry at my father for dying and leaving me. That was a popular interpretation at the time, but I wasn't able to develop those feelings of anger. Perhaps, I repressed those feelings. Or, in keeping with what I felt as a child, I simply may only have had feelings of love.

One month after my father's death, the Japanese attacked Pearl Harbor. People in California were afraid of possible attacks by airplanes and submarines. Listening to the radio, it felt like the world was coming to an end. I said to my mother: "It's a good thing my father died. He wouldn't have wanted to experience a Japanese invasion." I was serious. I thought, illogically, that his death protected him from a worse possible fate. With the death of my father and the beginning of World War II, my mother entered new areas of concern: fear, poverty, citizenship, and work. And, these changes affected my life as I continued to grow and develop.

6

Poverty

Months after my father died, my mother found that she was poor. She was not a citizen of the United States, and she feared the possibility of deportation as an Italian alien. Christina was not gainfully employed, and there was little money from my father's death benefits form the Western Pacific Railroad. Part of his benefits included a family railroad pass that could be used for traveling any place in the country. Our family used the pass to travel to Ithaca, New York. My brother, Joe taught me how to tell time on the train. And, in Ithaca we played games such as seeing who could drink the most glasses of salted water. I also traveled to New York City when I was a 19 year old Berkeley student. One memorable incident occurred when I was enroute from New York City to Berkeley. I left my seat in the train to sleep in the lounge where it was more comfortable. When I woke up I found myself alone in the lounge car. It was in the middle of a railroad yard in Green River, Wyoming. I managed to get to the train station and have the railroad people to call ahead to save my baggage. I guess I wasn't a very smart Berkeley student; and it was clear that even then I carried a lot of "baggage."

In 1942 my brother, Tommy, enlisted in the Navy, cutting short his baseball career; my sister married a man of Portuguese descent; and my brother, Joe, was away much of the time, gambling and planning to join the Merchant Marines. The upshot of this was that my mother and I were usually alone during World War II.

I didn't know we were poor right away. However, two events emphasized our poverty. During Christmas season, The Sacramento Bee, the evening newspaper, accepted letters from needy families requesting toys for their children. My brother, Joe, wrote a letter to The Sacramento Bee; and as a result, I received a toy sailboat which I played with at the McKinley Park pond. The toy made me feel rich, but it was the knowledge that Santa Claus made special trips to give presents to needy children that clued me in that we were poor. The second event was much more direct. My mother applied for relief in kind. I had to go with her to the welfare office so she could prove she had a needy child. We received a box of groceries after each visit to Mary Judge, the social worker. It was very clear, like her namesake, Mary judged whether or not we were eligible to receive relief in kind. Who knows whether those memories spurred me on to study social welfare, psychiatric social work, and social research in the years to come?

During those years, especially when I was nine to eleven years old, I seemed to develop mentally at a rapid pace. My third grade teacher liked me and thought I should skip the fourth grade, based on my third grade performance. I jumped at the chance because I liked being at school very much. I used to arrive an hour or so before school classes began, talking with a janitor, and warming up next to a wood burning stove. In the first grade I was not a good student. I didn't know how to read or write. At home the only books I looked at were comic books that Joe brought home. My mother read an Italian newspaper, and I occasionally glanced at the sports pages in The <u>Sacramento Bee</u>.

I was embarrassed in the first grade. The teacher, Mrs. Cunningham, asked us to write our names. I didn't know how to write, so she, accentuating my ignorance, asked another student to write my name for me. In that same class, I pronounced the word "criminal" as "CRIN-IMAL" everyone laughed. That simply spurred me on to do better. By the time I entered the second grade. I was up with the rest of the class, and I began to show a knack for spelling and arithmetic. By the third grade, I typically completed all of the assignments very early. For example, I did the year's assignments in arithmetic in the first month. My mother's reaction to my skipping the 4th grade is registered in this brief dialogue. "Hey Ma, the school is having me skip the 4th grade, so I'll be in the 5th grade," said I. She said, "That's ok as long as you don't get into trouble." That was the response of an immigrant with a third grade education from Italy. She was less worried about my education than she was about the potential embarrassment if I did get into trouble. Unlike the Chinese immigrants who enforced the importance of education for their children, it didn't seem to be a priority for Italians and Hispanics in Sacramento. I was the first one who would go to college. However, there was a rapid acculturation and almost all of my mother's grandchildren graduated from college.

To get off of welfare my mother appeared to have these choices: she could marry a wealthy man or find a job. She eventually remarried, divorced, and worked. In 1943 she married Mr. Mandella who had quite a bit of property, grown children, and a very big house. What most impressed me was that he had a white goat that give milk and ate everything that could fit in its mouth. My mother and I moved to his house. Nearby lived the Schiro family, of which one was a deaf mute. I got a Boy Scout book and learned the alphabet in sign language so I could impress him by saying something. "Where are you going?" is what I practiced until I had the courage to try it out on him. He smiled and spelled out "Work." I couldn't afford to be a Boy Scout, but I read Boy Scout books at the library. I read enough to satisfy in my mind that I could meet the basic requirements for an Eagle Scout. To this day I marvel at the American library system and its impartiality to the rich and the poor.

My mother almost immediately began to believe that Mr. Mandella was poisoning her. She spit out what she thought was poison, scratched her head, and swore at him. He appeared to be a moral man who spoke often about Christianity. In retrospect he reminded me of the preacher in Sommerset Maughm's story of Sadie Thompson in "Rain." The preacher was moral with respect to others, but he also had his own moral weaknesses and ambivalences. I thought Mr. Mandella was kind, and I liked him. Perhaps, I was seeking a father substitute?

The marriage didn't last longer than a couple of months. My mother and I couldn't move back to the house on 24th Street since it was being rented by someone else. Across the street from the house, a neighbor allowed my mother and me to live in the basement for a short period of time. It was a dark, unlit dirt basement. We slept on some makeshift furniture. There were spiders and spider webs and possibly other creatures. I was ten year old and afraid of the dark and the unknown. I was also angry at my mother for leaving Mr. Mandella and for having us live in the dark basement. It was supposed to be temporary. I, who desired instant gratification, didn't understand the meaning of "temporary." I was cold and frightened, and wondered when Christina would abandon me for throwing poison in her hair.

Soon we were back in the house on 24th Street. During World War II, there were many jobs for women who replaced the men in the armed forces. My mother got a job as a janitor at the Southern Pacific Railroad in the daytime, and in the evening she worked in a cannery. She would leave for work at approximately 6:00 a.m. and return about 1 to 2:00 a.m. the next morning. She was successful in working us out of poverty, and she began to save her money.

My mother, Christina, felt that she had to look young to keep her job as a janitor. Hence, she dyed her hair, not with a dye but with black shoe polish. That certainly would have led her to scratch her head! She worked hard and for long hours, essentially leaving me unsupervised and alone. She would leave the ingredients for dinner, and I would make something. I opened cans of beans and peaches; fried wieners or hamburgers; and made coffee. Not wanting to miss work, she left me alone when I was sick. One day I vomited, had a fever, and could hardly take care of myself. I felt alone and angry, and I vowed to myself as much as possible not to get sick again. And, for the most part, I don't remember getting sick again until I was a student at the University of California, Berkeley.

We lived near the railroad tracks, and bums would often come by our house, sometimes stopping to drink water from the faucet outside of the house. I was wary of most of them; however, there was one man who wore a black suit with a vest and derby hat that I liked. This is because he gave me a nickel, a 5-cent piece, and told me that I would live until I was 90. Even to this day, a man of 73, I believe that I will live until I am 90 years old, thanks to the prophecy of the bum who gave me a nickel. That was the optimistic view of bums. The downside was that I was afraid that some other bums would rob the house while I was in it. Consequently, every night that my mother worked at the cannery, I would play with friends until their parents said they had to go to sleep. Then, I would stand under a lamp post about a block from my house, waiting for my mother to come home. She was always surprised, but comforting, when she met me each working night at the lamp post.

There were two ways that I sought love during the early years of World War II: from a dog and from the Catholic religion. Christina obtained a dog for me, a reddish brown Australian Shepherd. I called the dog Toughy, probably because I wanted to be tough but wasn't. Toughy gave me unconditional love, allowing me to pet and cuddle him. During the summer months, for a brief period, Toughy was my companion. Unfortunately, Toughy bit someone; and my mother gave Toughy to a farmer who lived approximately 15 miles from our house. Just like in a scene from Lassie, Toughy left the farm and returned to me. The farmer retrieved Toughy and made sure that he'd never again escape.

The second way I sought love as a ten year old boy was to go to catechism classes at St. Francis Catholic Church, near Sutters' Fort in Sacramento. Different nuns were our instructors. A friend of mine, Leo, and I earned many religious medals by memorizing prayers. Of course, we didn't understand the words we memorized. And I felt terrible when a sister told us that dogs couldn't go to heaven. I simply couldn't understand why Toughy and I couldn't wind up in the same place after our sojourn on earth. I thought, perhaps wrongly, that one could pray for what one desires. I wasn't successful in having God return Toughy. Since I couldn't have Toughy, I prayed for a person to love me. This was a prayer I uttered through high school and college. The inconsistent love from my mother was insufficient. Obviously, I didn't understand the concept of being loved by Jesus, which is what I thought the Catholic priests and nuns professed to teach.

Ostensibly, I was a Christian; but I really wasn't, since I only thought of fulfilling my desires.

Christina did not seem to be very religious. There were religious relics throughout our house; however, she rarely attended church. When my father was alive, Christmas and Easter were important events. Not only did everyone go to church, we also ate many different kinds of meats, vegetables, fish, pastries, breads, and biscuits. Easter was a relatively happy time. I loved hard boiled eggs, especially the tasty yellow part. I suppose my mother could have claimed she was religious because she was born with religion in her genes. Her grandfather was a priest who gave up the priesthood to marry Christina's grandmother, who was a nun. To thank God for being acquitted of a serious crime, her grandfather built a church in the late 1800's in the village of San Pietro L'Apostolo (St. Peter the Apostle). Calabria, Italy. The church is still standing and is currently in use. I visited the church in 1980 with my cousin Vincenzo Grandinetti, a geometer in Calabria. At that time the church was closed, and the local priest had to wake up the drunk sacristan to have him open the church for a tour of the inside. Several Italians accompanied the priest, my cousin, the sacristan, and myself. It was extremely interesting to hear how they were very keen on understanding the intricate details of architectural construction. The most noteworthy event for me was the discovery of an embroidered blue table cloth on the altar. My mother made it and sent it to San Pietro L'Apostolo from California!

Christina didn't arrange for me to have a religious education; that is, planned communions and confirmations for which children dress in fine white clothes and have triumphant parties for achieving certain levels of belief in the Catholic church. I made communion by my own efforts. In catechism I learned what one was supposed to do to make communion. Then, I went to a confessional and confessed; afterwards I received communion along with other parishioners. My interpretation of sins was very strict. Any bad thoughts I had I interpreted as a bad action. Unlike Jimmy Carter, if I had lust in my heart, it was an act of lust, not a thought. Hence, I had to say many Hail Mary and Our Father prayers as penance. Little did I realize that the penance was variable and changed as a function of the confessor's interpretation as well as that of the priest. In later life, I became very lax and lenient in interpreting sins, perhaps to make up for all the guilt I felt when I was a child.

I took Catholicism very seriously. It was a pleasure to hear chants sung in Latin at high mass. I wanted to learn Latin, so I asked the nuns who lived in a convent across from St. Francis if they would teach me Latin. They said they would do so in exchange for my raking their lawn. However, they only taught me some prayers, not how to read and write Latin. My real opportunity to learn Latin had to wait until junior high school and high school. In addition to enjoying the priests' chants in Latin at high mass, I also was fascinated by their blessings. They sprinkled holy water on the parishioner. I had often wondered whether Christina imagined that was how people threw poison on her, i.e., by sprinkling the poison in her hair!

7

Citizenship

My mother, like other aliens in the United States during World War II—the Germans, Italians, and Japanese—worried about being put in a concentration camp or being deported. It was only in recent years that I learned from the novelist Lisa Scottoline that some Italian aliens were actually put in concentration camps, as well as the Germans and Japanese. Christina quickly decided that she must obtain U.S. citizenship. She enrolled in an evening class that included immigrants from a number of different countries. I went to the classes with her and tried to point out those things she had to remember: ages of those eligible to be president, the number of senators, the preamble to the U.S. constitution, and so forth, Christina quickly learned the essential facts; for she had a very good memory. Most of the questions from the citizenship students, all of whom were adults, resulted from their unfamiliarity with English.

Christina couldn't read or write English, but she could understand some words and could speak a kind of broken English-Italian. She pronounced the English words she knew in a unique Southern Italian style. For example, mashed potatoes were smash-a-na patate and vegetables were vege-ta-ba-lay. I felt very important in that class because I was helpful to my mother. I was in the sixth grade and was a good student who also liked to sing.

One day at Marshall Elementary School I was called to the principals' office. I thought I was in trouble, but I didn't know what I had done. It turned out that a teacher and Mrs. Von Hatten, the principal, wanted to hear me sing. I complied by singing a popular song at the time: "You are always in my heart even though we're far apart. I can hear the music play the song of love I sang to you…" They agreed I had a mature voice for my age, and they encouraged me to sing in school functions. However, I was deeply disappointed when I didn't get the part of the prince in a musical play, <u>Sleeping Beauty</u>. I was told I was too dark for the part; the prince was supposed to be fair skinned. This, of course, led me to be ashamed of my dark skin. My siblings also told me was I too dark. They suggested I wash myself thoroughly every day, and my skin would turn to a lighter color. I wished I were blonde and blue eyed. I practiced hard for the part and thought (maybe it wasn't) my voice was excellent. I learned that looks appeared to be more important than the actual sound of the voices in the musical play. Perhaps, it was sour grapes, but I became disinterested in singing at school; I became sensitive about my dark skin.

I lied about my age in order to be eligible to have a newspaper route. I was one year younger than the required age, but the newspaper staff didn't ask for proof. I had two routes to deliver The Sacramento Bee. One was in a working class section of town; the other was in a downtrodden, part of Sacramento with alcoholics, pimps, prostitutes, drug abusers, and very poor people. Collecting the monthly bills was an adventure because I never knew if in turn I would be robbed.

I had an old bicycle, and it was virtually useless. Most of the time, the rear tire was flat. I was constantly trying to patch the inner tube of the tire, but to no avail. I'd fill the repaired tire with air; and, in about 15 minutes it would be flat again. Obviously, I frequently walked the newspaper routes. My eyes were opened to a seamy side of life. Some customers were half naked; others were drunk. Many of the apartments reeked with awful smells. I received no tips and felt I was lucky to collect the money the customers owed. Nowadays, papers are delivered by persons who drive cars, and the payment of bills is centralized and not the responsibility of those who deliver the newspapers. The good news was that I did make some spending money. I used some money to watch movies on Saturdays at the Alhambra Theater. Usually, I'd watch a couple of cartoons, a movie, the news, and an episode of a long running serial such as The Lone Ranger.

Christina and a friend of hers, Rosa, picked strawberries on weekends for extra money. I tagged along and picked a few strawberries, eating more than I picked. Rosa and my mother worked the hardest among the workers. They picked the most strawberries and earned the most money. Rosa was always first, and Christina was second. I also worked on farms in the summer of 1944. I'd go to the skid row in downtown Sacramento to try to get work for one day. The skid row was full of homeless and unemployed men. Along with others, I'd wait for a truck to come by, with the driver asking for workers to pick hops. Rarely did I get selected to hop on the truck. Mostly men and a few teenagers were picked. Picking hops was hard work, I was paid several dollars and I received a hot lunch for a day's work. I used the money to buy a sweater. I learned from my mother to work hard and fast, and not to think of anything else. Maybe I learned to focus on whatever task I was involved in from her. And, perhaps, when she worked hard and fast, she was less plagued by her delusions.

Between the sixth and seventh grades I was less frightened than in previous years. It stemmed from the fact that I was getting bigger and that I stood up to my mother. She continued to badger me about throwing poison in her hair. When she became angry, she tended to strike out, to slap, or to spank. Often she'd say that she was going to kill me. One day she came to me with a knife. I wrested it from her and knew I wasn't going to let her hit me any more. Yet, I always wanted to know where she was physically, especially when she was angry. This was a turning point in my development. I was more conscious of my physical strength, and I realized I could protect myself. However, it was still difficult to protect myself from the words that were hurled at me. I learned to talk back to her and to avoid any crazy talk by running off to play.

Christina did become a United States citizen. She continued to dye her hair with black shoe polish, and she became aware of her health problems. She was a diabetic and had to self-administer insulin shots. She asked me to give her shots, but I was too squeamish about needles penetrating skin to do it. Christina was supposed to follow a strict dietary regimen, but she couldn't do so. She preferred to eat pizza and dunk fresh bread in wine. She might have made one of the first wine coolers by mixing wine and a 7-Up soda.

My mother used the wine press that my father left behind to make wine herself. She supervised me and any of my friends who were nearby to squeeze the juice out of the grapes. Like my father, Christina made three barrels of wine per year. She drank several glasses of wine each day, but I don't remember her ever getting intoxicated. At times, I went down to the dirt basement where the wine barrels were stored to take a few sips of the strong red wine. It had a much higher alcoholic content than wine that was sold in the stores. My mother also kept beer in the ice box, and I tasted it with her approval. My father, Nick, drank Buffalo Beer, and I probably tried to emulate him.

My father was a citizen of the United States. He studied plumbing, hoping it was a trade he could learn. He valued his U.S. citizenship. When he worked, he always made sure that he would send money to his mother in Italy. As an immigrant, he dreamt that his son would become upwardly mobile in the American class system. He wanted me to be a civil engineer. I had no inclination to do so. However, every summer during my college years I was employed as an engineering assistant in the state of California, the Army Corps of Engineers, and the U.S. Geological Survey. Perhaps it was a surreptious way to please his memory. These jobs paid fairly well, enabling me to save some money for college.

8

Delinquency

I was eleven years old in the seventh grade at Sutter Junior High School. At first I was a good student since I already knew the seventh grade material. Mathematics and spelling were my favorite subjects, probably because I did well in them. I tested at the high school level in them when I was in elementary school. I didn't want to go to Sutter. I wanted to go to a different junior high school that was academically oriented. It was also in a nicer neighborhood. I lived in a different area and was not allowed to transfer schools. Hence, my junior high school days were to be spent at Sutter, which euphemistically was called a "crime school." It was worse than that! Many students skipped school, stole cars, fought with knives and fists, and were impudent and sassy. Student activities formed a catalogue of different criminal and delinquent acts.

As time passed, I too became a sassy, impudent delinquent. This probably began when I stood up to my mother and didn't allow her to hit or spank me any more. The memory of that event apparently sparked my delinquency. A foreign language teacher was angry at me for being sassy. She slapped me in the face, and I quickly slapped her back. The result of this was that I earned 800 minutes of detention, time that I had to spend after school with other students who were in trouble.

Since my mother had two jobs and my siblings were away most of the time, I was essentially unsupervised. It was war time, and there were curfews for juveniles. However, I didn't stay home. Instead, I often went downtown, two to three miles away, to play pinball machines. I became fairly proficient, winning lots of extra games. My brother, Joe, bought a pinball machine and kept it at home; and I learned to tilt the machine in a way such that it didn't register tilt. This was obviously good training for tackling the downtown pinball machines.

I began to be involved in delinquent acts with other boys, partly out of companionship to dispel my feelings of loneliness. My brother, Joe, was involved in gambling on horses, poker, and shooting craps. He dropped out of high school in the eleventh grade just when I started the seventh grade. One might say that was our "seven come eleven" period, the luck of our draws. A mathematics teacher, Mrs. Best, praised me in front of the class, saying how smart and nice I was compared to my brother Joe. He evidently turned a fan on in the classroom that blew papers helter-skelter all over the classroom. Mrs. Best did not realize it, but her statement was interpreted by me as an invitation to prove that I could be worse than my brother Joe. At the very next examination, as she left the room, I let everyone copy my paper. Mrs. Best did not feel like she was the best when she discovered that everyone scored 100 percent on the text. She believed our class was full of trouble makers who were not adept in mathematics. When the opportunity arose as she left the room, events like this recurred. She eventually found out it was nice Tony that was the culprit. The story was promulgated that she was so upset by this discovery that she decided to resign. She might have wanted to resign anyway. I, at the time, thought it was funny knowing that I had demonstrated I could be just as bad as my brother. In retrospect, it was very mean and callous of me to take revenge on her for putting down my brother. That event, however, served as a continuing sign that I was becoming more and more delinquent.

My friends and I went out at night to steal. There were many blackouts; the lights were turned off and the streets were pitch black. This enabled us young hoodlums to ransack cars, taking what was available, primarily from glove compartments. Most of the cars were not locked. Occasionally, someone would catch us in the act, and we ran and hid. We especially thought it was thrilling to hide from and escape the police. We also pilfered ice cream and milk from a cannery, and, almonds from an almond factory. I didn't like milk, but somehow it tasted better when stolen; perhaps, it was the lure of "forbidden fruits." We had many close calls, and later we actually were caught stealing from a store. In the summer we stole tomatoes from a field on our way to swim in the American River. It was somewhat frightening when a farmer shot at us. We ran, deciding that we really didn't need to pick juicy, red beefy tomatoes. In essence, the shotgun extinguished our tomato stealing behavior.

I stole from my mother as well. She gave me money to buy her some medicine, typically Ben Gay for arthritis. I'd steal the medicine, and keep the money. Ironically, I now use Ben Gay to alleviate some of my arthritic pains. I suppose, had I known that I would be arthritic as well, I would have kept the medicine and given the money back to my mother. My mother never knew I was involved in stealing from the store and from her. More than likely it would have made her very angry. Although it wasn't right for me to steal from the store, I then thought it was ok to take the money from my mother because I satisfied her need for the medicine.

My friends and I did not have a variety of new clothes. I usually had clothes that my brother wore. To obtain new clothes, we stole from department stores. We would try on some clothes, and walk out without paying. For example, I'd go to the boys' clothing section of a store wearing a jacket. Selecting a sweater, I'd put it on in the changing room and cover it with my jacket. Then, I'd nonchalantly stroll out of the store. If I were caught, I would have said I forgot to take it off. The key to successful stealing was to put on the sweater when no on was looking.

One friend had a job at a drug store. Several of his friends, including me, helped him to steal whiskey. He eventually was discovered stealing, and he had to repay the owner for what was stolen. He didn't tell the owner that others were also involved. It wasn't planned, but I eventually paid him back in a small way. His brother and several of us were involved in stealing merchandise from a Payless store. We often taunted the store detective by pretending we stole something and walking around and around inside the store with the detective following us. We knew it wasn't technically stealing until we left the store. When we did go outside, he nabbed us. He was furious when he discovered we didn't have any stolen goods. This teasing behavior was sadistic on our part. In one sense it was metaphorically similar to the teasing I received from my mother; however, she was probably not aware of her inconsistent talk, i.e. "teasing," with me. Christina spoke with love like expressions on the one hand ("Ti voglio bene, mio figlio." I love you, my son.), but on the other hand would withdraw her love, shouting she would kill me for throwing poison at her.

One day we got caught stealing key chains by the detective. He wanted to know whose idea it was to steal the key chains. The idea originated with the little brother of the person who stole alcohol from the drug store. There was silence. Nobody wanted to take responsibility. Finally, I said it was my idea. The other boys were given a warning, and I was taken to a police station. Eventually, I was released with a warning that I would go to reform school if this behavior continued.

My stealing behavior stopped in the ninth grade, not because I received help from anybody and not because I came to my senses. Basically, I discontinued stealing for two reasons. First, I confessed my sins to a priest at St. Francis and received a penance of hundreds of Hail Mary's and Our Father's. More importantly, I was frightened by the priest's depiction of the wrath (not the mercy) of God. Second, I discovered sports. I played football basketball, and ran on the track team. Sports occupied my time, whereas I was not interested in academic subjects. In the classroom I was regarded as a hopeless brat. I had women for the academic classes and men for physical education and team sports. I was well behaved in the classes I had with male instructors but had difficulty with women instructors. Perhaps, I had little respect for women due to the interactions I had with my mother. Whenever a group of kids that included me were in some kind of trouble, I was always singled out as the leader (which I wasn't). I wore dirty corduroy pants and a white t-shirt most days, and I was darker than most of the kids I hung around with. I was often called a "dirty Mexican." I definitely wasn't a dirty Mexican. If I were labeled as a "dirty Italian," I might have had slightly more respect for those teachers.

I excelled in sports. I was relatively fast and played half back, offensively and defensively. In basketball I specialized in snaring rebounds and taking long set shots. In track, I ran the 50 yard dash and the 600 yard run. Our teams were not very good, but I enjoyed traveling to other schools and being involved in the physical aspects of sports. It was especially enjoyable to be excused from classes to play games at other schools.

I also became involved in the band and the orchestra. I played solo trombone, but sometimes I substituted for others, playing percussion instruments. My pre-dilection for sports over music as well as my lack of responsibility was evident in this example. I was walking from my house to play in a concert at school. The first piece was Tchaikovsky's first symphony for which I had the introductory solo. On the way I saw I saw some friends playing basketball. I put down my trombone and decided to play for a few minutes. I became so involved that I played for about an hour. Realizing I was late, I ran to the concert. I got there too late to play the solo part. The orchestra director, Mr. Scott, a very mild-man-nered man, who frequently rubbed his hands with lotion, gave me a cold stare, which lasted throughout the evening and into the following semester.

It was then that World War II came to an end. My friends and I went down-town to join in the celebration. Many were drunk, and everybody was kissing and being kissed by joyous, strange women. As one might expect, my relationships with girls in junior high school were very guarded. There was a girl in the neigh-borhood that loved to kiss experimentally with several of us. Her name was Jeanie, and like the song, she did have light brown hair. About four houses from her, an older girl, Mary, frequently had people to her to house to engage in sexual intercourse. I didn't, but my brother Joe did.

I had no steady relationship with any girl then. Doris, who played cello and was reputedly the prettiest girl in the ninth grade, gave me her ring, telling me we were going steady. I liked her, and I accepted the ring. However, I was shy with girls, and I didn't even pursue talking with her. Several weeks later, I walked with Gwen to a school event. Doris was very angry and demanded that I return her ring, which I did. Through no action on my part, I was supposed to be going steady with Doris. Then, I was supposed to have broken up with her. Somehow this made me popular with other girls. However, I didn't date any girls, nor did I have intimate relationships. I felt I was unattractive because I had acne and was not able to keep it under control. Upon graduation, I was voted as having the best looking hair, but I wasn't aware of it. Although I acted tough in the role of juvenile delinquent, I was, in my mind, very soft, sentimental, and vulnerable. This aspect of my developing character was something I wanted to hide. In spite of the fact I felt unattractive, I knew some girls were attracted to me due to my exaggerated toughness. I was not attracted to them. I preferred shy, intelligent girls, but I didn't talk to them either. I thought of interpersonal relationships as musical comedies with romance in the air and a song in my heart. I kept those thoughts to myself except for Vanetta, who was two years older than I. Like a misguided romantic, I actually sang a song to her. Of course, I was rejected. She was interested in having money spent on her, and I didn't have money to spend. I liked older girls perhaps because they seemed more maternal. And, it was maternal love that I craved; if not from my mother, then from older girls!

In some ways I did get some respect from my delinquent friends. I took beer from home and put it in my locker so that I could display how tough, manly, and carefree I was. The truth of the matter was that I was very stupid. Fortunately, I wasn't apprehended by school authorities. On days when the entire class chose to skip school, we shared beer and sodas while swimming at the American River. Another stupid act in which I was engaged was making gun powder with another boy. It was my first introduction to chemistry, and I found it interesting to think about the formation of compounds. Unfortunately, my friend had his finger blown off; and, fortunately for me, I decided to stop trying to make explosives. Had the accident not occurred, we would have explored the possibility of making a more powerful explosive, nitroglycerine.

My mother had no idea that I was involved in delinquent activities. My brother, Joe, was probably aware, but he never said anything about it. He seemed to know everyone, including the reputed head of the C Street Gang, Jack Brady. He most definitely was not one of the Brady Bunch. He was a boxer, and along with other members of the C Street Gang was into armed robbery, fighting, and drugs. Jack was feared by many people. In contrast, he had a kind streak. In elementary school, I pretended I could fly by jumping off of different places, like the roof of our house. Movies like Superman and Captain Marvel went to my head. One day I jumped off a baseball screen and caught my foot in it so that I fell on my arm, breaking it. Jack, who lived across the street from the baseball park, came to my assistance He took me to the hospital. He said he knew my brother, and he was glad to help. Jack and most of the C Street Gang wound up in prison!

My best friend, Dick, and I were the only ones who did not receive outstanding citizenship awards upon graduation from the ninth grade. I acted as though I was proud of not being a good citizen, but I really felt ashamed. A couple of teachers told me I would never make it in high school. I had no expectations other than that I wanted to play sports. I never discussed academics with anyone at home. Like my siblings, it was probably expected that I would graduate from high school and obtain a job in the local community.

As a 14 year old, high school sophomore, I lost my bravado and feigned toughness. I was preparing for a new phase of my life. My mother accumulated money, and she was buying, fixing, and renting houses that she bought. She seemed to have a knack for making good decisions about real estate. She didn't talk about suicide anymore; however, she continued to believe that people were trying to poison her. I became embarrassed whenever a friend came to my house. Christina would whisper to me in Italian about the foul smells and the poison in the air, while spitting in a handkerchief. My friends didn't understand Italian, but whenever Christina talked about poison, it felt like she was announcing to the world on a loudspeaker that I was poisoning her.

9

High School

The direction of my life quickly changed in high school. This was a result of two events. First, I was told that I had the ability to do well in college. In the high school in which I was enrolled, there were three classes of students on the basis of aptitude tests: Z, the slow learners who were expected to work in a trade; Y, those who were expected to attend college; X, those who were expected to excel in college. Accordingly, classes were arranged in difficulty depending on whether the students were categorized as X, Y, or Z. Expectations for classroom performance were the highest for X students and the lowest for Z students. If X and Y students were in the same class with the same difficulty of an examination, X students had to achieve more points than Y students to receive the same grade. For example, an "A" for a Y student would have been a "B" for an X student. I tested as an X student; and my counselor encouraged me to think about college. It was the first time I ever thought about going to college.

The second event had to do with sports. I had ingrown toenails, and I was told by a podiatrist that I would no longer have the problem of ingrown toenails if I had operations on my feet. Dr. Matheny operated, but the operation was unsuccessful. My big toes were swollen. I had a second operation, which again prolonged the time before I could play football. I was anxious for my feet to heal rapidly. Stupidly, I played basketball on a gravelly playground, when my feet were supposed to be healing. My toes became infected. When they did heal, I discovered that I couldn't run as fast as I once did. I played a little football at end, but the position I really wanted to play was running back. My feet hurt off and on in my sophomore and junior years. The basketball coach offered to build me a special shoe that would have been ostensibly more comfortable, but I refused since I was in too much pain. A good part of the time I was in limited gym rather than on a sports team or in physical education classes. Later, I discovered the podiatrist was a quack and lost his license due to malpractice. My mother accepted whatever Dr. Matheny said as gospel, and I didn't know any better.

I loved sports. However, it became clear to me that I definitely was not slated for stardom. This was painful, for I imagined that I was a good athlete, especially in football and basketball. In pickup tackle games that a group of us played every Saturday at McKinley Park, I enjoyed running with the ball, trying to elude tacklers. Although I played and lettered in football, I was not a good football player. I performed better as a guard in basketball. Scheduled to be a starter, I was beset by another injury. I broke my finger, and I was not able to play through the pain.

Those two events, aptitude testing and sports injuries, led me to think more about college. I had many discussions with Mr. Kimball, and he indicated I could receive scholarships if I performed well in my classes. He was a humble, meek man who gave me a powerful message: "You can do well in school, and you can graduate from college and be employed in a profession." He thought I had an aptitude for science, so I took courses in physiology, chemistry, physics, advanced algebra, trigonometry and solid geometry as well as the standard courses in English, History, and a language, Latin.

By the end of my sophomore year, I changed my habits so that I studied constantly, doing required and extra homework every night for all of my classes. In a sense, this also gave me an excuse to avoid family arguments with my mother and her new husband, Charlie Bartucco. He was an alcoholic, and he smoked Tuscan cigars that really stank. Charlie certainly gave my mother good reason to say he was poisoning her with cigar smoke. They both drank many glasses of red wine, and they argued every night. With my new interest in academics, I was able to say, "Shut up. I need to study." That worked, and they toned down the noise level of their arguments. When my mother yelled to me that he was throwing poison at her, I said, "I can't talk about that now. I need to study to get through school."

I was obsessed with studying. Not only did I want "A grades," I also wanted to score the highest in examinations. I achieved this in physiology, science, chemistry, physics, and Latin, but not in other subjects. I thought science courses were interesting and important, while history was not, with its emphasis on memorizing dates rather than discovering thematic patterns in different eras. I made two new friends. They were interested in chemistry, desiring to become professional chemists. Bob later earned a Ph.D. in organic chemistry from the University of Illinois, and he obtained many patents regarding the chemistry of drugs. Dave became a chemist in industry. I, in contrast, received my doctorate in social research from the Columbia University School of Social Work.

Bob and I created the S and T (Scherrer and Tripodi) Laboratory in the garage at his house. We conducted a variety of experiments for fun. Bob planned and built a seismograph, which helped to earn honorable mention for him in the National Westinghouse Science Competition. My experiments with ultraviolet to affect the growth of plants were not successful. In the school's competition for the Bausch and Lomb Science Award, I was first and Bob was second. Upon high school graduation we all received scholarships to attend the University of California, Berkeley, but we deferred matriculation at Berkeley to attend Sacramento City College for a year, thereby saving some money.

I became increasingly distant from my mother in high school. I was working at scholarly subjects to have a chance to get away from screaming, yelling, and accusations about poison. I was callous and inured to my mother's feelings. At the same time, she actually became nicer apparently wanting me to achieve my goal. Christina was supposed to be on a strict diet to control her diabetes; however, she couldn't stick to it. She had glaucoma and her eyes were getting worse. She often had dizzy spells, and she was affected with chronic arthritis. For relief of her aches and pains, Christina spent hours soaking and sleeping in the bath tub.

The only way I could study at home was to suppress my feelings of anger and block out the noise from the nightly arguments. "Why did they have to argue every night?" was a question I asked often, but which I suppressed in order to study. Sometimes tears would come to my eyes, and I had to force myself to snap out of it. In a sense, I was only studying to escape the pain of listening to arguments between Charlie Bartucco and my mother. I probably did well in school because I studied more than most people. Although my mother was making more money, I did not receive an allowance. I quit my newspaper routes to concentrate on studying. However, my brother, Joe, often gave me money for doing chores for him, such as washing his car.

I joined a number of honor societies becoming president of the National Honor Society (California Scholarship Federation) and the Science Honor Club. An issue of money arose when I asked my mother to give me money to purchase a pin for a membership in the History Honor Society. My brother, Tommy, said that he never got any pins in high school. Smart ass that I had become, I said, without knowing whether it was true, "That's because you weren't smart enough." It was very insensitive to say that. Only recently Tommy told me that he had to work throughout high school, and he gave most of the money he earned to Christina. He was a great football and baseball player, but couldn't play due to his working hours in selling and delivering newspapers. He is one of the nicest people I ever met. His world has always been consumed by sports. Playing professional baseball with minor league teams, he always batted over 300 averaging 20 home runs per year. After he retired from professional baseball, he played semi-professional baseball for the love of the game. As he became older, he umpired baseball and refereed basketball games for high school, college, and recreational teams. Tommy worked in warehouses and in maintaining baseball parks. He is devoted to his wife, Vera, and his daughter, Tina, who obtained a degree in landscape architecture from the University of California, Berkeley. Tommy was honored by being named to the Baseball Hall of Fame for both Sacramento and Stockton, California.

Although I was appointed Attorney General of the high school student body and belonged to all of the honor societies, I didn't engage in any of the potentially fun activities. I didn't dance; so I didn't go to proms, nor, did I routinely date. Occasionally, I'd go to a movie with male friends, but not often. Unrealistically, I'd attend church on Sundays praying for and hoping I'd meet the girl of my dreams. I went out once with one girl, Diane. She and I were partners in chemistry working on experiments on different reaction times in the formation of compounds. After a movie, we went to her house, and I kissed her. The next day in school it seemed like everybody knew. I was embarrassed and not wise about the phenomenon of "kiss and tell." This reinforced my feelings of not trusting females, and I withdrew further from them. Obviously, I had little experience with women, and I was immature in interpersonal male-female relationships. Perhaps, this is a legacy from my mother; it has haunted me throughout my life.

My mother divorced again. There was too much dissension in the marriage. She was not happy at all. Their evening meals were laced with wine, shouting, swearing, and multiple accusations. Charlie was a different man when not drinking, with a nice smile and a look of caring when he spoke to me. He had a daughter in her 20's whom he loved very much. It appeared that he married my mother because she had more money than he did. After the divorce, my mother and I moved to one of her houses next to Tommy's house. I was so wrapped up in my studying that I hardly interacted with her except for dinner. She had stopped working, just caring for the property she purchased, ordering my sister, Phil, and brother, Tommy, to help her in managing and maintaining her houses.

She directed much of her anger toward my brother, Joe, who was a bookie and a gambler. Joe made a great deal of money, but he gave her very little. Christina banished him from her house. She again exhibited the pattern of anger, withdrawal of love, and total rejection. Years later, Joe taunted her with a similar pattern. He asked Christina if she wanted to go to Italy, while he was holding a thousand dollars in bills. She said, "Yes," while she tried to grab the money. With a sadistic grin, he burned it. A couple of months later to make up for his sadism, he gave her enough money to take a trip to Italy. In that trip, her relatives robbed her of money and possessions, and she was very disappointed.

I continued to excel in school. As president of the California Scholarship Federation Chapter in my high school, I traveled to other schools interested in starting chapters of the honor society. I was especially thrilled in giving a speech to the student body of St. Francis High School. It was a girl's high school adjacent to St. Francis church, where I went when I was in elementary school. That area was always peaceful; it included the church, Sutter's Fort, and a park with a small pond and ducks eagerly awaiting bread crumbs.

My counselor, Mr. Kimball, was always available for advice. I spoke to him about preparing for the college aptitude tests, which, at that time, were the Iowa Quantitative and Linguistic Tests. High scores in the quantitative section were supposed to be indicative of success in science and mathematics; while high scores in the linguistics section were indicative of success in English, history, and foreign languages. Mr. Kimball suggested I read novels to improve my vocabulary so that I could better answer questions about vocabulary, synonyms, and antonyms, and word analogies. I told him there wasn't enough time to do that, so I would memorize lots of words and their meanings. I did extremely well, scoring at the 99th percentile for both quantitative and linguistic portions of the test. I didn't hear it, but I was told that Mr. Kimball spoke about me in a radio program. He talked about my interest in college and my success in grades and aptitude tests. If the program served as a feather in his counseling cap, I believe it was well deserved. Despite my family circumstances and my errant background, it was he who encouraged me to do better for myself through education.

A question for which I don't know the exact answer is, "Why did I do well in school?" According to the book, Growing Up with a Schizophrenic Mother, by Brown and Roberts, 44 children of schizophrenic mothers had difficulties in interpersonal relationships, had few close friends, and were ashamed of their mothers' behaviors. However, they were all relatively successful. Perhaps, they, as volunteers were accomplished in their professional lives; whereas, those who didn't volunteer for the study might have been less successful.

Christina plagued me with her paranoid delusions, and I was extremely immature in interpersonal relationships. Yet, I developed a strong will, a willingness to succeed at whatever I endeavored to do. This was most certainly a trait I inherited from my mother. She succeeded despite her delusions by finding a way to control them so they didn't interfere with her major tasks. In a similar fashion, I was able to control the demons of my mother's sickness and my fear of becoming crazy by intellectualization and blocking my feelings from entering the tasks on which I was focused. I was not a complete person. I acted like I was devoid of feeling, had tough skin, and was mentally strong. In truth, I was anxious, vulnerable to criticism, and unsure of myself in social situations. And in later years, I would discover that I had only suppressed the demons of my youth and that they were still there to haunt me in the way I thought about myself and in the way I related to people.

10

College

I first matriculated at Sacramento City College. It had the same freshman and sophomore courses as the University of California, Berkeley; so I was able to transfer them as well as save some money in the process. I was probably at the height of my intellectual powers. I felt confident, choosing the toughest classes I could find. The first semester I took engineering, chemistry, calculus, German, English composition and rhetoric, English literature, and physical education. I worked hard, receiving the highest grades in all of my classes. I had no social life. I only studied and exercised in physical education. I found that I could run again, and I enjoyed playing touch tackle football and basketball. The basketball coach saw me play pick up basketball games, and he asked me if I would like to play on the basketball team. I was flattered and considered it, but then turned down his offer, continuing to devote my time to academic classes. In the second semester I studied qualitative analysis in chemistry, advanced calculus, scientific German, physiology, and philosophy.

It was in philosophy that I met Carlton Garske, who came from a different high school than I did. He also introduced me to another friend of his, Glenn Housh. Both of them were reputed to have extremely high I.Q.'s, in the 160's to 180's; and they were perennially goofing off, horsing around, and mocking the life around them. In philosophy class, Carlton noted that another student sat by us when quizzes were given, and he copied from our papers. To stop that, Carlton suggested that on the next quiz we put down all the wrong answers, wait until the copy cat left, and then change our answers to be correct. We did this, and the copy cat failed. Moreover, in the calculus class, Carlton suggested after a midterm examination that we act like we failed. After the examination we kicked lockers, made a noisy fuss, indicating it was the toughest examination we ever took. This made some of the students a little anxious since we were known to be good students. As it turned out, I had the highest score in the class; while Carlton had the second highest score. Now I can see that these taunting and teasing behaviors were reminiscent of my mother and my brother, Joe.

I did not date girls at Sacramento City College. I occasionally saw a movie or a sports game, and I continued to attend church at the Cathedral downtown, praying for that love that was nowhere in sight. In accordance with mental health researchers who pointed out that patients had fewer symptoms and mellowed as they aged, my mother also had fewer delusional episodes. She became very supportive, keeping me well fed and allowing me time to study quietly at home. She appeared to be content that I was working hard at my studies.

The Korean War was taking place. Carlton joined the U.S. Navy and became a cryptographer, while Glenn, David Lofing, Bob Scherrer, and I prepared to become students at the University of California, Berkeley. I received a State of California Scholarship a Sacramento City College Scholarship, and an award for having the highest grape point average. The Korean War was in full swing, and all of us took draft deferment tests so that we could continue in college without being drafted. Ultimately, David and Bob were not drafted due to physical maladies; Glenn spent time as a clerk typist in the Army; and I was a journalist in the Navy.

The University of California, Berkeley, was only 80 miles from Sacramento; however, in political and philosophic orientation it was light years away. There was a great tolerance of diversity and different cultures in Berkeley. Students openly discussed communism and socialism, and they skeptically reviewed Asian and Western religions. There were people from all over the world, and there was a great intellectual fervor. There also were radicalized students who tried to upset hearings of the House Committee on Un-American Activities; and professors orated about why they would not sign loyalty oaths. The atmosphere was intimidating because all of the students appeared to be bright and very worldly.

To travel home to Sacramento I hitchhiked. My mother made care packages of salami, pepperoni, parmegiano reggiano, and anise flavored biscuits. My scholarship covered tuition, room, and board. However I had to work at different jobs to earn money for clothes and extra food. The transition to Berkeley was difficult. I became more and more distant from my family but did not easily adapt to the living situation. I was housed in a cooperative building where everyone had to work several hours per week, I was assigned to live with others that I didn't particularly like; and the noise made it difficult to study. I became very anxious, and I was not able to study in an efficient manner.

Hitchhiking was an adventure. Sometimes I got picked up by lonely people who bared their souls. Some rides were bizarre. Once I was picked up by a husband and wife who were drunk; and they talked to a parrot, and I couldn't wait to leave. When I wore dressier clothes, I seemed to be picked up by people in nicer cars. In contrast, when I was sloppily dressed, I rode with truck drivers. I also hitched rides in the Navy. Then, I had to be alert for drivers who were looking to have sex. Although I didn't date at that time, I wasn't a homosexual. I knew my family might have thought I was gay, but I wasn't. I simply was very immature with very little experience with females.

Bob introduced me to Teresa my first semester at Berkeley. She lived in San Francisco, and she was a student in our high school class in Sacramento as well. I fell in love with her and engaged in kissing but nothing else. I believe she was disappointed in me because I didn't' try to have sex with her. I also thought she was dating other men. My beliefs were tenuous. It simply might have been my inexperience that bothered her; I really didn't know. I was obsessed, and I began to skip classes. This was very difficult, especially in organic chemistry laboratory where one had to be very patient, putting in long hours to achieve the results of an experiment. I became anxious about my ineptness at interpersonal relations, and the anxiety spread to my studies. I started to worry about whether or not I was crazy. This led me to switch majors from chemistry to psychology. And why psychology? I was more interested in learning about myself than about other people! The relationship with Teresa fizzled. Soon after, I started a relationship with Jane. She too was a graduate of Sacramento High School. I met her at the public library in Sacramento. We became friends. It was a platonic relationship with no sexual activity involved. She spent some time studying fashion design in New York City before returning to Berkeley to study French. With a railroad pass I visited her in New York City, wore my first suit that was handed down by my brother, Joe, and discovered that I was very naïve about life, especially in New York. Jane and I became companions at Berkeley in my senior year. We weren't lovers, but we acted as boyfriend and girlfriend.

Our relationship soon changed. My best friend, Carlton Garske, was released from the Navy, and he matriculated at Berkeley to study literature. I spoke very highly of Carlton to Jane, and of Jane to him. The result was that they immediately became attracted to each other. They became lovers, and I was devastated. I trusted both of them and felt I was betrayed. This reinforced my distrust of women. Memories of not trusting my mother pervaded my thoughts. I avoided Carlton and Jane, and I took a trip to visit cousins in Los Angeles. When I returned, I joined the Naval Reserve, planning to serve on active duty after I graduated.

I was an honor student at Berkeley, but I didn't achieve the best grades. I didn't work as hard as I previously had. I was not sure of what I wanted to do, and I was extremely apprehensive about the future. In the library at Berkeley, I sometimes thought I would lose my mind. I would stare at my books and feel a flood of thoughts meshing in my brain. I felt like screaming but didn't. I would leave the library and just walk around. I couldn't concentrate. I smoked three packages of cigarettes per day; and the more I smoked, the more anxious I became. I felt that I lost my intellectual capacities as well. Ironically, it became clear that my mother actually provided a protective environment for me in high school and at Sacramento City College. And, away from that environment, I was flooded with anxieties from my youth.

I concentrated in Abnormal Psychology. Unaware of Christina's diagnosis of paranoid schizophrenia, I studied the symptomatology of schizophrenics and other major psychiatric categories. I felt very uncomfortable when observing paranoid schizophrenic patients, but I didn't relate their behaviors to my mother's delusions.

Before I matriculated at Berkeley, I radically changed the course of my life. I was an engineering assistant for the U.S. Geological Survey in Elko, Nevada. At the instigation of Carlton Garske, I read fiction. Prior to that time I only read scientific books. I read a book a day. I was 18 years old, a romantically challenged adolescent. I began to day dream about sex, love, and adventure.

Bob Scherrer and I were at the same camp, assisting in surveys of the Nevadan hills. One of the engineers was a P38 fighter pilot in World War II, and I was astonished when he talked about how he had strafed women and children. He was a little crazy, putting his truck in neutral, racing down the hills, pretending he was flying a P38. Reading a book each day opened up my thinking but also increased my anxiety. The work we did, recording elevations, was relatively precise. Reading novels led to an exploration of new thoughts and ideas, and I carried this activity with me to Berkeley.

At Berkeley, I spent a great deal of time in cafes. I was ignorant of political, sociological, and economic perspectives. Yet, I learned different points of view by listening to people expound their theories over coffee. Reading novels and art books spurred me on to write poetry. I wrote dozens of poems about chaos, love, and serenity. I wrote my first poem while sitting on a green, grassy hill on a lazy, warm day: "I dream a dream of thoughts where eternity exists in unblemished imagery…" My poems were sophomoric; however, I poured my heart into them. I gazed at the stars and wrote about lonely people. I also discovered the world of classical music. I played records over and over. Rachmaninoff's Second Piano

Concerto was beautiful, but it always depressed me. I wrote poetry while listening to it. I understood that the composer was recovering from a bout with depression when he wrote the music. My poetry seemed to engender anxiety and depression. I wrote about the sky, oceans, and the stars, but not about real people with real feelings. I never wrote about my mother and my family. Before I graduated I threw away all my poems. They were gone, but anxiety and depression lingered. Perhaps, the Navy would be a positive experience.

11

The Navy

I joined the Navy, not to see the world but rather to meet my obligation to serve in the armed forces. Since I was deferred from active duty for a couple of years, I felt that it was necessary. It was also a way to avoid Carlton and Jane. I idealized the Navy because my brother, Tommy, seemed to have had interesting duty in Australia during World War II. I didn't want to enlist in the Army, so I thought of a way to enter the Navy. I applied to Officer Candidate School and was accepted. Reasoning that if I flunked out, I would be assigned to boot camp and have only two years of duty instead of more than three as an officer. Basically, I had a history of dizziness and nausea in land, air, and sea vehicles. That is, I had motion sickness. And, I really wasn't sure the Navy was for me. However, I felt my chances of survival were greater.

At Newport, Rhode Island, I enjoyed history and navigation, but not seamanship and gunnery. Again, I found that I couldn't concentrate on my studies when I lived with several other people. The upshot of this was that I was near flunking seamanship and gunnery. I liked the Navy uniforms, but I couldn't see myself supervising others in gunnery. I had a difficult time visualizing the mechanics of large guns. After two months, I decided that I would quit. And, for one of the few times in my life, I consulted my mother. If she wanted me to become a Navy officer, I would have kept plugging away. I thought the prestige was important for her. I was wrong. She said she was only interested in what was comfortable for me. She was very supportive, allowing me to quit with no guilt feelings whatsoever. However, I did have some pangs of regret when I was told that I was slated to be a naval attaché in Naples, Italy, due to my background in Italian. It was a better choice for me to spend 22 months on active duty instead of 3 ½ years!

I was assigned to boot camp at Bainbridge, Maryland. It consisted entirely of discipline and physical exertion. I didn't have time to be anxious or depressed, nor did I have time to think. I simply focused on keeping my uniform and my living space clean. Because I scored high on the intelligence tests, I was chosen to assist the drill instructor in teaching the semaphore code. There were African Americans, southern whites, Italian-Americans, Hispanics, college graduates, high school dropouts, and those who cared little for themselves or others. Often times there were racial tensions, primarily between Southern whites and the few Blacks that were in the company. The Italian-Americans from New Jersey and I sided with Blacks (African Americans), helping to avert fights.

The discipline helped me to obtain a better perspective on my future. Hard and consistent work seemed to be a good work pattern for me. There were some amusing times in boot camp. For example, in an inspection, a commanding officer with white gloves was known to be a stickler for clean shoes. As we were lined up, a pigeon flew by defecating on a sailor's shoes. When the officer came to that person, he stepped down and rubbed his white gloves in the pigeon shit. He quickly realized what had happened, and he moved on. We had to hold our laughter until inspection was over.

One Italian-American tried to be a matchmaker, introducing me to an Italian American woman. Unfortunately, we didn't match at all, and it was clear she was already attached to someone else. My friend had good intentions but was completely clueless about Connie.

After boot camp, we were to be assigned to different schools, depending on our interests and aptitudes. I chose journalism school on the presumption that I would probably be assigned to a land base, rather than a ship. Of course, my presumption proved to be incorrect.

Upon graduation from boot camp, I felt very sure of myself. I was not bothered by the demons of anxiety, depression, and the fear of going crazy. The journalism school was at Great Lakes, Illinois. Students were from the Navy, Air Force, and Marine Corps. We were instructed in various facets of the newspaper business: photography, layout, news reporting, tape recorded interviewing, magazine writing, and so forth.

If we did well in our assignments, we were granted liberties off base. This was a great incentive, so we worked hard so we could visit Chicago. I enjoyed going to the Art Institute to view paintings by the great impressionists. We sailors roamed in groups, and we seemed to have spent a lot of time going from bar to bar, drinking and laughing. Some of us wound up at a Walgreen's Dug Store. One sailor bet me that I couldn't get a date with any girl sitting at the soda fountain. Since I thought (the new me) I was sure of myself, I accepted the bet. The other sailor, George, also had to try to pick up a girl. He approached a girl, blurted out that he wanted a date with her, and was completely rejected. I approached who we thought was the prettiest girl there. She was Mexican. I asked her if I could have her address so I could write to her and ask her to see a ballet. She gave me her address. I wrote to her, and she accepted a date a couple of weeks later. I went to her house but discovered that I wasn't simply dating her. I was dating her and her five brothers. Under their watchful eyes, I was very polite and unassuming. We didn't date again, but I did win the bet with George!

Journalism school lasted three months. Usually, graduates in journalism would be assigned to naval bases, i.e., shore duty. Our class evidently was the first class where all the sailors were assigned to ships. I did have a way to obtain shore duty, however. I knew a sailor who was on the U.S.S. Wasp. It was in Japan, and it was slated to go to Hunter's Point in San Francisco for maintenance and repairs, i.e., dry dock. In other words, the Wasp was to be in San Francisco for approximately seven months. With that knowledge, I accepted assignment to the U.S.S. Wasp.

The students at journalism school were fairly verbal. There, like in boot camp, were some tensions regarding race and sexual orientation. One African American student was openly homosexual, and some of the other students teased him. One student form Ohio, who I called Bucky, in particular, was full of prejudice. I told Bucky that, perhaps, the reason he was so antagonistic was that he, himself, might have been a latent homosexual. That made Bucky angry, but he did quit his teasing; perhaps, affirming that he wasn't a latent homosexual.

The Marines acted as if they were tough. I played basketball for the school, and it was very clear that it was more like football than basketball. Of course, we sailors had to show we were just as tough as those Marines. As a result, there was much shoving, bumping, and fouling.

I flew to Yokuska, Japan to go aboard the U.S.S. Wasp. Prior to returning to the U.S., I enjoyed liberty in Kamakura, Japan, the site of a large Buddha. It was beautiful and very interesting to hear the music, to learn about Japanese drama and to see scrolls of paintings that had floating images. I was especially taken with a Chinese lullaby sung in Japanese.

The U.S.S. Wasp stopped in Hawaii and then docked in San Francisco. During that time I reconnected with Jane. Carlton married another woman, Mary. Jane thought I was more mature, and we became lovers. We were married after I was released from duty in the Navy, but we didn't really talk about my feelings of betrayal. Perhaps we should have because eventually I betrayed her.

After dry dock, the U.S.S. Wasp was stationed in San Diego, and we went to sea for one or two weeks at a time. There were two journalists and approximately 3,000 other sailors. We wrote short news items for the sailors' hometown newspapers, and we produced a newspaper for the ship. We wrote sports and feature stories. Upon discharge, I was asked if I wanted to re-enlist and run a radio station in San Diego. I, of course, refused; for I thought the Navy was extremely dehumanizing. One sailor who was in charge of keeping watch over an area was always teased because he was mentally slow. He was asked, "What time is it?" by sailors who knew he couldn't tell time and who laughed as he stumbled in trying to come up with the correct time. Prior to discharge from the Navy, I applied to graduate school, specifically social welfare at the University of California, Berkeley. One friend of mine told me about psychiatric social work, thinking that it would be an interesting career to pursue. I thought I'd give it a try, but I wasn't too sure about it as a career choice. I was happy that I was leaving the Navy and planning to live a married life with Jane. We did not have sexual relations in our courtship thinking that we would explore that after we were married. I would be in graduate school, receiving money from the G.I. Bill; she would be continuing her studies in French; and we would live in student housing. We were married in a Congregational church in Sacramento.

Upon leaving the Navy, I felt more mature and decisive. I didn't' think of my mother's psychosis. My brother, Joe, was becoming prosperous. He was a restaurateur and a bookie. He divorced his first wife, Mary, and married Janice. Joe employed family members to work in the restaurant that he partly owned. The pattern of multiple marriages for him and for me was just beginning. We learned well from our mother! Meanwhile, my sister, Phil, was taking care of Christina, our mother, who had glaucoma and was blind. Phil had a large special room and a separate bathroom for her. Christina was sad about her blindness, not being able to see her grandchildren and not able to read the Italian newspaper. She had mellowed considerably and was unhappy about her health. I tried walking around the house with my eyes shut just to imagine how it would be to be blind. It could not have been easy for my mother, for it was difficult for me after only a few minutes with my eyes shut.

12

Graduate School

It felt good to return to Berkeley with a positive attitude for studying. I again became a serious student, excelling in classes dealing with law, social research, social and psychological theories, and social policy. It was more difficult for me to do well in social casework, where the class focused on discussing feelings of social workers and their clients. My internship in the first year of study was at the Marin County Department of Public Welfare. Marin was a very wealthy county near San Francisco. Within Marin County there were pockets of poverty. One such pocket was in Marin City where most of the residents were receiving public welfare. It was difficult work because there was a culture of poverty among the residents. They appeared to believe they were entitled to receive money from public welfare without trying to find jobs. Many of the women who received benefits hid the fact that they had husbands or boyfriends that lived off of them. The men avoided being seen by public welfare workers. Had their presence been detected, the eligibility of the women for benefits from Aid to Families and Dependent Children would have been in jeopardy. The giving of cash instead of food relief in kind, which my mother received, allowed more freedom for the recipients to plan their lives. Social workers often helped the clients to budget so they could adequately meet their needs. Of course, the best made plans were disrupted when some clients spent their money on liquor to share with their boyfriends.

My supervisor felt that I was technically correct in the way I thought about and worked with clients. However, she felt I was stilted, mechanical, and not creative in the way I dealt with feelings. Nevertheless, I felt my work was good. There was a state survey of public welfare clients who showed they were making movement or progress. One of my clients was among the very few clients in the entire agency that showed movement. The client, Mrs. J., had constant headaches. I didn't ask her how she felt about her headaches; I simply asked her if she needed glasses. She had her eyes tested, and it turned out she needed glasses.

Wearing glasses, her headaches disappeared. I was probably lucky in that I acted on a hunch, and it proved to be correct.

The prize for first year students was to obtain a psychiatric internship for the second year of the M.S.W. (Master of Social Welfare) program. I applied for and received a placement at the Veterans Administration Neuropsychiatric Hospital in Palo Alto, California. There were many advances taking place there, by renowned physicians, psychiatrists, and psychologists. The Veterans Administration had its first anthropologist there as well as the innovations of behavioral modification. In addition, there were studies of ataractic drugs, double bond theories schizophrenic families, and so forth. Moreover, our students had consultation from both psychiatrists and psychologists. The additional incentive for obtaining psychiatric internships is that they also provided financial subsistence. At the end of the first year, I was feeling good about myself, doing well in academic work, and looking forward to the second year.

I did begin to worry that I might not be cut out to be a good social worker since I didn't seem to easily discuss my feelings. Little did I know that it would be a problem for me at Palo Alto. I went to the Berkeley Counseling Services to receive aptitude and interest testing regarding future careers. It turned out that I retained my interest in science and in working in scientific activities. My aptitudes were thought to be suitable for work in medicine or in Ph.D. programs. According to the results of the Concept Mastery Test, a test devised to predict success in Ph.D. programs. I performed two standard deviations higher than the typical doctoral students in all fields at Berkeley, i.e., above the 99th percentile. The counselor recommended that I study medicine. However, I didn't even like to look at blood, and I was squeamish when receiving shots. I remembered that I couldn't give insulin shots to my mother for her diabetes. I gave blood once for my mother. When the blood was withdrawn, I felt faint and somewhat sick. I became very interested in social research in the social work program and tried to pursue more courses in that area. However, I was the only student that was interested.

In the second year, students were exposed to psychological and psychoanalytic theories. Those courses were taught by psychiatrists, psychoanalysts, and psychiatric social workers. Almost all of the students were in psychotherapy. It was recommended as a learning device. I was one of the few who were not in therapy. The atmosphere was one of sexual activity. There were affairs between students and students, and apparently between students and professors. I attended most classes in the second year with Elsie who was also placed at Marin County Public Welfare in the first year. We engaged in a brief affair, and that essentially broke up my marriage. I don't know whether I initiated the affair or was seduced by Elsie. I certainly was naïve. The result was that I felt I betrayed Jane. I was an adulterer, and I felt I should be punished; so the marriage had to end. And, in retrospect, I don't know whether or not I was taking revenge on Jane for having betrayed me to be with Carlton years ago. If true, that would have been a distortion of the Italian vendetta. I felt despondent and anxious, and it affected my work at Palo Alto. I felt anxious seeing clients, and their psychiatric symptomatology was frightening. My supervisor saw that I was anxious and not feeling well. She was kind, and she suggested I seek a therapist with whom I could discuss my problems. I told her I would think about it. The next day I told her I decided not to seek therapy for myself. For some reason, that made her angry, and she became cold and abrupt with me. Whenever I'd ask a question in group discussions pertaining to research, she'd publicly say that my questions were inappropriate. My supervisor's switch from being kind to acting coldly was reminiscent of my mother's inconsistent behavior. My session with the supervisor was stressful. She kept on pushing me to discuss my feelings with clients, and she tried to get me to relate them to my family. I didn't comply. I thought my family was my private business. However, in retrospect, it was clear that she was trying to be helpful; if I could have understood my feelings, it was presumed that I would understand the feelings of others as they related to me. I did do well in co-leading groups. I was able to cognitively understand the ramblings of some psychotic patients and their free associations. This helped me to lead the group to achieve its goals.

There was a conference regarding my performance, and the supervisor and the school of social welfare liaison person decided that I should pursue research rather than directly working with patients. As a consequence, I attended the same seminars as did psychiatric residents. Moreover, I was assigned as a research assistant to two projects: one was conducting experiments on learning; the other was concerned with evaluating the effectiveness of psychiatric services. My performance was good because my anxiety subsided, and because I enjoyed research activities. I was offered a job as a research social worker at Palo Alto upon graduation, but I turned it down in favor of a job as a research technician for the California State Department of Mental Hygiene.

Word got around about my divorce, and one of the students at Palo Alto indicated her interest in me. She was married and had three children. Again, I didn't know what I was doing, and I became involved with her. She separated from her husband, and she accepted a job as a social worker in Sacramento.

Hence, my post graduate career was to return to Sacramento and work in research. It was also to return to my mother and to see her for the last year of her life. And, it was to discover my strengths and weaknesses as a human being. After my mother's death, I entered the doctoral program in social research at the Columbia University School of Social Work. Upon graduation, I began a 42 year career teaching at a number of universities: Columbia, University of California, Michigan, Pittsburgh, Florida International University, and The Ohio State University, of which I am now Dean and Professor Emeritus. I did well in my work, but I continued to struggle with interpersonal relationships, continually distrusting others.

13

Postcript

There is no doubt that my mother, Christina, had a great influence on my life. This is what I learned about her and her influence on me:

1. My mother was diagnosed as a paranoid schizophrenic by the California Department of Mental Hygiene. Her main symptoms were that she believed people threw poison on her, and she had to expectorate to rid herself of the venom. She became angry when she displayed her symptoms, withdrawing her love from whomever she believed was poisoning her.

2. She was able to control her olfactory hallucinations of foul odors and her tactile sensations of poison being thrown on her. For most of her life, she was a hard and fast worker. She was able to acquire and save money, making sound investments in real estate. This was done despite the presence of her demons. One way she controlled her symptoms was to speak about them only in Italian, not in English; hence, English speaking people who didn't understand Italian would not hear her accusatory words about poison.

3. Christina had multiple marriages. It appeared that she drank wine a great deal, argued with her husbands, and said they were poisoning her. Just as she did with my brother, Joe, and with me, she loved and withdrew her love in an inconsistent manner. Ironically, both Joe and I have had multiple marriages, largely due to immaturity in relationships with the opposite sex.

4. Over time, Christina became less angry and she rarely displayed her symptoms. She was beset by advanced stages of diabetes and this gave her great pain. She also mellowed and became consistent in showing her love to her grandchildren.

5. She taught me to focus on a task despite any anxieties or illness I might have had. In her work she was in a hurry to pick the most strawberries, can the

most peaches, buy the most houses, etc. Correspondingly, I have always completed tasks, such as writing articles and books, quickly. I wanted to finish an examination first, be promoted the fastest, complete a book in record time, and so forth.

6. Christina didn't seem to trust people she worked with, and she didn't trust her husbands. She may have had good reasons to be distrustful; however, her inconsistent love influenced me to distrust her. I distrusted love and affection from others.

7. At times, I thought I would be crazy. This made me very anxious and hesitant to interact with other people. My mother's inconsistent love-hate relationship with me occurred when I was very young, and I did not understand that her erratic behavior was a result of her mental illness.

8. Except for the occasional influence of my brother, Joe, I had no reliable male role model when I was growing up. The positive influence of Mr. Kimball, my high school counselor, is an example of how a consistent role model might have influenced me to be a better person. For example, I might not have engaged in delinquent activities as frequently as I did.

9. It is very clear that Christina had a very difficult life as an immigrant in America. She was forced into a marriage she didn't want, and she worked in her early years in America essentially as a slave dominated by her husbands. Yet, she was successful in making the world a better place for her children. She loved us, and she made our lives better through her efforts. We took advantages of opportunities she helped to create for us. I knew she would have been most proud to know that her son is included in the prestigious Marquis', <u>Who's Who in America</u>.

My mother did not receive psychiatric care and treatment throughout her life, with the exception of a thirty day observation period when I was very young. In retrospect, I believe these recommendations might have been helpful.

1. My mother probably would have benefited form drugs that could have controlled her symptoms. Such drugs may have induced her to be angry less often, perhaps, resulting in more positive interpersonal relationships.

2. Christina's children might have benefited from psycho-education, i.e., education about her mental illness and the meaning of an attempted suicide. Books and pamphlets about mental illness would have been useful.

3. She might have benefited from a family services agency focusing on her relationships with male partners and her children. In the long run, this could have been as helpful as the relief in kind which we received.

4. I could have benefited from counseling by a strong male role model; for example, from a Big Brother volunteer, a school social worker, or an interested teacher. Instruction about the value of education and the pitfalls of delinquency would have been informative.

5. During periods of anxiety, I might have been helped by participating in support groups; for example, male children of mentally ill mothers and delinquents with immigrant mothers.

6. Individual therapy would have helped me to deal with the expression and handling of my own feelings about family problems.

The above recommendations are indicative of attempts to involve family members in understanding and dealing with mental illness. There still is much stigma attached to those that are mentally ill. It is especially difficult for immigrants and their families to be open and revealing about mental illness. Throughout this short volume I have tried to illustrate the positive and negative influences my crazy, Italian mother has had on my life. Perhaps, this poem epitomizes her influence on me as a child and as a young man:

My Crazy Italian Mother

Sitting in a chair with the TV turned on,
My mother reminisced about her childhood
In Italy.
Although blind, in her mind's eye,
She viewed the crystal clear waters
Of the Mediterranean Sea.
The demons in her head swirled
Around and around,
Like the eddies of the American River
In which she wanted to drown.
Thinking I threw poison on her,
She spat on the ground,
Releasing an invisible venom
I never found.

I felt pity as she kept company
With her companions.
Her sadness touched my soul,
And I wondered whether my thoughts
Would flow
Into the whirling world
Of her delusions.

978-0-595-39607-8
0-595-39607-0